THE PATENT OFFICE
Department of Trade

A Century of Trade Marks

A commentary on the work and history of the
Trade Marks Registry, which celebrates its
Centenary in 1976

LONDON
HER MAJESTY'S STATIONERY OFFICE

ISBN 0 11 511719 9

Foreword

The Centenary of the Trade Marks Registry, which first opened its doors on 1 January, 1876, comes at a turning point in its history. After many years of relative stability, both in the law and practice of trade marks, the Registry is entering a period when its work will be influenced much more than hitherto by international developments. This book is an attempt to give the background to the establishment of a statutory system for protecting trade marks, the way the system has worked in this country and a look at what the future might hold. It gives a glimpse of the activities of the Registry and of some of the personalities who have worked in it. Trade mark law and practice is commonly seen as a mysterious and esoteric subject, comprehensible only to the expert, for whom much has already been written in works giving detailed and authoritative information. I hope that this book will fill a gap – providing the general public with a readable layman's guide to the basic principles which have governed the registration of trade marks over the last 100 years.

The book has been prepared by the Assistant Registrar, Mr R L Moorby, with assistance from Mr D G A Myall and Mr F J Ward Dyer of the Registry. We are indebted also to others who have carried out research and provided information about the history of the Registry, particularly Mr James Harrison of the Patent Office. Most of the references to early trade marks in Chapter I are derived from a paper read before the Institute of Trade Mark Agents by Mr J G C Ruston in 1953. We are grateful to him and to the Institute for permission to use them.

We are all constantly meeting trade marks in the advertising media and using them for choosing the goods we purchase. A recent survey has shown that trade marks are of considerable significance and value to housewives, in relation to the goods which they purchase week after week. Yet few who put their trust in trade marks realise the full significance, and limitations, of those marks. I hope that this book will not only provide some useful information in that direction but also create a wider interest in a subject which is important alike to the consumer and to those engaged in industrial and trading activities, both in the home and export markets.

E Armitage
Comptroller-General and Registrar of
Trade Marks
March 1976

Contents

I *Early Trade Marks*

Whether a mark on goods is a trade mark depends on the use to which it is put. When goods are sold in association with a mark intended to indicate who made or sold them, the mark becomes a trade mark. Most of the early marks on goods fall into the two categories of makers' or owners' marks. A mark simply to indicate possession of an article is not a trade mark; nor, in general, is a maker's mark, such as an artist's signature on a painting. But a maker's mark may acquire the characteristics of a trade mark, even if it is not normally so regarded, and although the article itself (such as an original painting) may be unique, provided that the article is made the subject of commerce. Thus the signature of an artist whose paintings are traded in is in principle a form of trade mark, and to this day a signature used as a trade mark is regarded as distinctive and may be protected at law.

Most of the oldest marks known are on pottery; because pottery tends to survive longer as an artefact even than stone and many metals, and marks on it remain discernible almost indefinitely. Possibly the oldest marks of all are those on some pottery jars found in Transylvania and made perhaps as long as 7000 years ago. It seems on the whole unlikely that these were true trade marks, but the interesting thing about them is that the way in which the marks were formed, by combinations of straight lines, remained for many thousands of years (certainly well into the 16th Century) characteristic of many marks which were undoubtedly true trade marks. Marks similar in style to Transylvanian ones, whether or not true trade marks, were used throughout the ancient civilisations of Egypt, Crete, Etruria and Greece.

It is not until we come to Ancient Rome that we can be sure some of the marks on goods were true trade marks. A good many of the thousands of known Roman potters' marks can be attributed with assurance to certain identifiable workshops. Moreover, these were early instances of word marks, though usually in conventional form – for example, CATIM (Cati manu: from the hand of Cato), and OFALBIN (officina Albini: the workshop of Albinus) – whereas earlier marks had been almost invariably devices or ideographic symbols. Roman pottery was evidently sought after in Britain, for there are various examples of filching of goodwill by imitation both of the goods and of the marks. Imitation Roman pottery was made in Belgium in the early part of the 1st Century AD, before the Roman Conquest of Britain, and exported to this country. Some of it, bearing imitations of Roman marks, is in the British Museum. Presumably as a result of their ignorance of the Latin language, the Belgian imitators succeeded only in creating meaningless collections of letters, but the bogus marks seem to have deceived the still more ignorant Britons. In Rome, where there was a highly developed commercial law, a purchaser of goods thus fraudulently marked could bring a civil action, but there appears to have been no civil action open to the true proprietor of an imitated mark.

During the Dark Ages the use of trade marks seems largely to have lapsed, though, as the name of the period implies, we have little reliable information. An exception was the marking of sword blades. Blades were manufactured in the Rhineland for several centuries during this era and exported all over Europe. They bore makers' marks, which, because they were on articles made for sale and must have brought the makers some goodwill, were in fact trade marks. The British Museum has an example of a late Saxon sword of about the 10th Century which bears a trade mark consisting of ornamental matter and the word INGELRI, Ingelrius being a well known swordsmith of the time.

From the 12th–13th Centuries onwards the use of trade marks on a variety of goods spread rapidly. The medieval merchants of Norwich, about whom a good deal is known, provide many examples. They used their marks not only as true trade marks, but also as personal marks (in lieu of coats of arms, the right to which was limited at that time to land owners). Some of these marks can still be seen today on their houses in Norwich and Yarmouth. Printers' marks also began to be widely used from the 15th Century. William Caxton, the first English printer, took the mark 'W. 74.C', in reference to the year 1474 when he started printing, and this was almost certainly a true trade mark. In important commercial centres, such as the Hanseatic towns, merchants' guilds maintained their own registers of both local and foreign marks. The value of this practice is illustrated by the story of three merchants of Majorca who, as long ago as 1332, were able to prove their ownership of certain packages of wax, salvaged in Flanders from a shipwreck, by identifying their trade marks on the bales.

In Germany in the 16th and 17th Centuries there was a fairly comprehensive code of trade mark law, and a German author of this period wrote: 'No-one must take another's mark, even if he artificially disguises it by some addition, but keeps the principal part unchanged. As, for instance, a heart contrasted with the same heart pierced by an arrow.' In France, too, where there may have been no actual code of trade mark law, there is at least one recorded instance in the 16th Century of what would be called today a passing-off action, in which the defendant was subjected to a perpetual injunction and made to pay heavy costs. This punishment was not quite as severe as that suffered 200 years earlier in Germany by an inn keeper who sold inferior wine as genuine Rudesheimer. He was summarily hanged. In that case trade marks hardly entered into it; it was more a Trade Descriptions Act matter. The penalty is not only one more instance showing how we have changed our attitude to law-breaking over the centuries; for, though an isolated case, it also illustrates the fact that, as in France in the 16th Century, when the penalty for falsely marking cloth of gold was death, the law in those days was more concerned to punish deception than to uphold the rights of the owners of trade marks.

With the usual exception of the Dark Ages in Western Europe, compulsory marking to indicate the origin and often the quality or standard of goods was fairly widespread from the days of Roman Byzantium, 1400 years ago, to the Middle Ages and beyond, and of course continues today in the compulsory hallmarking of gold, silver and platinum. These marks were and are, however, only partly, if at all, true trade marks; their main purpose has always been to make it easier to trace the origin of sub-standard goods and often, particularly in the case of precious metals, to indicate their specific quality.

Up to the 19th Century the rights accruing to the owner of a trade mark, insofar as they were recognised at all, were derived almost solely from actual use of the mark, that is to say from the goodwill built up by its use. One exception in this country was the granting of marks for certain metal goods, first (from 1554 on) by the Court of the Lord of the Manor of Sheffield, and subsequently (from 1624 on) by the Cutler's Company. We know of only two other instances, before the Trade Marks Act of 1875, of the acquisition of rights in a trade mark by grant rather than by use. In 1571 R Matthews was granted Letters Patent to make hafts for knives and to mark upon them the device of a half-moon. In 1623 James I granted Roger Jones and Andrew Palmer a patent for hard and soft soap, which included the exclusive right to mark upon the goods or their containers a rose and crown, and also entitled them to enter, 'with assistance of a constable or some other officer', any premises where they had just cause to suspect that their mark was being counterfeited. Such a right of entry can be obtained today only on application to the Courts, and then only in the most exceptional circumstances.

II Origins of Trade Mark Law

A trade mark is a kind of shorthand symbol used to indicate the trade origin of goods. That is a truism so often repeated that it hardly seems worth stating it again. The practical advantages of using a shorthand symbol rather than the full name and address of the maker or supplier of the goods are obvious. A symbol is easier to remember and to recognise, and often easier to mark physically on the goods themselves. So, for the trader eager to have his goods sought out in preference to someone else's, and for the customer wishing to buy 'the same again', trade marks evidently serve a useful purpose. Nevertheless a question arises. How could such a complex edifice of common law and statute law as now exists in this country have been constructed on such a simple foundation? The answer lies essentially in the need, certainly felt during the past 100-150 years, to protect what has always been regarded as the natural right of any trader to maintain the goodwill in any true trade mark he has made distinctively his own. But this right does not mean that trade marks have always been regarded as assignable and transmissible personal property. Apart from Cutler's Company marks (see Chapter V), which in later times were transmissible to the owner's widow, it was not until the Trade Marks Registration Act of 1875 that trade marks were given statutory recognition as assignable and transmissible prop-

erty. This is where trade mark law differs radically in principle from patent law, the prime impetus for which has always been the social desirability of encouraging invention, and from the Merchandise Marks Acts and the relatively recent Trade Descriptions Acts (which are concerned primarily with preventing and punishing commercial deception and scarcely at all with the rights of owners of trade marks).

The principles of trade mark law are simple, but their application in disputed cases is frequently not, because elucidation of the facts is often difficult, the facts themselves are often complex, and each of the thousands of reported cases has its own special features. Since each decided case is taken as a precedent in deciding analogous cases, there is ample scope for elaborate legal argument. Until the 1875 Act, every plaintiff had also first to prove that his mark was distinctive in relation to his goods, for, if it was not, there could be no trespass on it. All such cases therefore tended to be lengthy and expensive, and by the middle of the 19th Century they were cluttering the Courts and delaying other work. The situation was aggravated by the great upsurge in the use of trade marks during the third quarter of the 19th Century – probably the climactic years of the country's commercial and industrial predominance following the Industrial

Revolution, and of course the years in which the effects of the Great Exhibition of 1851 were most widespread.

In 1862 there was an abortive attempt to introduce legislation on trade marks, but the Select Committee which considered the Trade Marks Bill of that year decided not to recommend it to Parliament. There appear to have been three main reasons for this. First, there were still doubts about the wisdom of conferring, by the mere act of registration, a property right in a trade mark which could be assigned to another party, for it was feared that, if the mark had acquired a repute in the hands of the first registered owner, its assignment would deceive the public as to the trade origin of the marked goods. Second, deliberate copying of valuable British marks, though widespread, occurred less at home than in foreign countries, and it was assumed that, in the absence (except for France) of reciprocal treaties, registration at home would be of no avail elsewhere. Third, it was felt that registration would not offer sufficient advantages over or in addition to existing common law rights to justify the expense and procedural inconvenience to trade marks owners. Nevertheless, commercial pressure in favour of statutory protection for trade marks persisted, and thirteen years later bore fruit in the Trade Marks Registration Act of 1875. The important difficulty concerning assignable property in a trade mark was met in the 1875 Act (but not in the 1862 Bill) by allowing a registered mark to be assigned only together with the business goodwill in the goods for which the mark was registered. This provision was continued in all subsequent trade mark legislation until the passing of the current Act in 1938. It was to administer the 1875 Act, which was enacted on 13 August 1875, that the Trade Marks Registry was set up in London, with a branch office in Manchester. In addition to recognising a statutory right of property in a registered trade mark (registration being 'deemed to be equivalent to public use') and establishing a register open to inspection by the public (so that traders could see whether a mark they were using or proposed to use was likely to come into conflict with a registered mark), the Act conferred a right to sue for infringement of a registered mark simply on the basis of a certificate of registration, thereby eliminating the need for a plaintiff to prove that his own mark was distinctive of his goods. Distinctiveness had therefore necessarily to be a condition of valid registration. But the 1875 Act failed to establish any formal criteria for distinctiveness since, apart from 'a written signature or copy of a written signature or copy of an individual or firm', each category of marks defined as qualifying for registration was merely required to be 'distinctive'. So it was left to the registration authority to decide, without specific guidance, what was or was not distinctive. Although later Acts have attempted to set rather more specific criteria of distinctiveness as regards word marks, the Registrar has still to decide in the first place whether or not a mark is distinctive, though as the years have gone by he has been increasingly helped by a long series of Court decisions.

The first Act had to take account of marks which had been in use before it was passed, so that some flexibility of criteria was probably inevitable. Word marks were not allowed under the 1875 Act unless they had been in use before the Act and were 'distinctive' (for what that requirement was worth, which was very little at that time). But inevitably a great hotch-potch of marks was sent in for registration – about 10,000 in the first year of operation of the Act, excluding cotton marks applied for to the Registry's Manchester Office. By no means all of these had been in use before the Act. But many of the word marks which were in use before the 1875 Act, and which were registered by virtue of it, would have been regarded by later standards as quite non-distinctive. Some remain on the register to this day, and most of them, even if not really 'distinctive' in 1876, have probably since acquired factual distinctiveness by continued use. However, the requirement of distinctiveness as a condition of registration was, at least in principle, written into the 1875 Act, and distinctiveness has remained a condition in all subsequent Acts.

Distinctiveness, however, does no more than render a mark suitable for registration. The underlying purpose of all trade mark legislation from the 1875 Act onwards has been – apart from establishing and maintaining a register open to public inspection – to offer the trader the opportunity (registration, remember, is not compulsory) of obtaining statutory recognition of a property right in any 'distinctive' trade mark without first having to prove that the mark, by virtue of use, exclusively identifies the owner's goods. Registration is subject to the proviso that the mark is not deceptive. There are two principal ways in which trade marks can be deceptive: by suggesting, by word or device, that the goods for which they are used possess characteristics which they do not; and by being identical or easily confusable with trade marks, registered or not, used by other traders for the same or similar goods, or indeed, in the case of very well known marks, for quite dissimilar goods. In neither case, particularly the second, need there be any positive intention to deceive. It is the fact, not the intention, of deceiving that both common and statutory trade mark law have sought to restrain. That infringement may occur without intent to deceive was firmly established in this country in a leading case in equity as long ago as 1838 (Millington v Fox). Deliberate deception by intentional copying or imitation of another's mark still occurs from time to time, particularly (so far as British marks are concerned) in some foreign markets, but the practice was a good deal more widespread 100 years or so ago. The British cutlery trade in particular suffered greatly about the middle of the last century when inferior foreign-made cutlery with marks of high-quality British goods was offered at lower, and sometimes even at higher, prices than the genuine products. This not only reduced sales of the genuine British goods but, more important, eroded faith in their quality and value. Intentional deception of this kind, however, has always been a matter for the Courts to deal with. The Registrar's main concern – once he has found a mark to be distinctive – is to ensure that there is no possibility of inadvertent confusion between it and other marks and to reject it also if it 'speaks' deceptively.

Until the 1875 Trade Marks Act, trade mark law as such hardly existed in this country. The many hundreds of cases involving trade marks which came to the Courts in the years before were brought, fought and decided under the heads of fraud, deceit, misrepresentation, forgery and so on, all of which were grounds of action either in equity or at common law. The first and

perhaps the most beneficial result of the 1875
Act was to reduce the number of these actions.
At the same time, the mere fact of the existence
of trade marks legislation probably – though it
would be difficult to prove – acted as a deterrent
to deliberate copying of marks, at least in this
country. At all events there appear to have been
fewer complaints of copying after the Act than
before. But the Act was only a beginning. It
needed improvement, even though most of the
basic principles underlying it remain valid, in
fact and in law, today.

III *Development of Trade Mark Law*

Meaning of a trade mark

English statute law concerning trade marks has maintained a remarkable consistency over the hundred years since its foundations were laid in 1875. This is perhaps not surprising as statute law in this field was firmly rooted in equity and common law (which dealt with many trade mark cases long before there was any legislation on the subject) and it retains close links with common law today. For example, the public's conception, as distinct from the lawyer's conception, of what a trade mark actually is was quite clear and accurate before the Act of 1875. In evidence before the Select Committee considering the 1862 Trade Marks Bill a witness who had no professional connection with trade marks was asked what his idea of a trade mark was. He said: 'A trade mark means the name, emblem or device used by any person to denote any article of manufacture to be the manufacture, workmanship, or production of such person, and serving to distinguish the products of one manufacturer from those of another. It does not mean a word, or name, or common denomination, descriptive of quality or quantity.' This is essentially what, with elaborations and different wording, statute law says today.

There was in fact no comprehensive statutory definition of a trade mark until the Act of 1905; the earlier Acts had left the definition to be inferred. The point is of some interest because it would clearly have been impracticable to legislate about trade marks, while omitting to define what constituted a trade mark (as was the case in the Acts of 1875, 1883 and 1888), unless the legislators were confident that the public had a perfectly good and clear idea of what a trade mark was. This confidence was not misplaced, as the lay definition quoted above shows, but by 1905 the tidymindedness of parliamentary draftsmen and the need to clarify some legal uncertainties led to the inclusion of a statutory definition in the Act of that year. In its essentials that definition is almost identical with the one in the current Act of 1938.

Requirements of use

The most important legal point cleared up by the 1905 definition related to use of a mark as a prerequisite of a valid registration. The definition specifically included marks 'proposed to be used'; though the Courts have held that this means that the registrant must have a 'present intention' to use the mark and not intend merely to put it in mothballs awaiting a suitable commercial opportunity to use it. The earlier Acts, which, as we have seen, included no positive definition of a trade mark, had stated that registration was to be deemed 'equivalent to public use'. This provision, which was carried forward from the 1875 Act into those of 1883 and 1888, iilustrates the closeness of the links between the early statute law of trade marks and common law. Under common law, a trade mark had to be in use to exist as such at all, so that the notional equivalence to public use which the 1875 Act attributed to registration in effect reflected Parliament's intention to make the new legislation an adjunct to, rather than an extension of, common law principles. Reported court cases in the early years after 1875 show that the judges were aware that the new legislation deliberately set out to give rights of title in new and unused marks; but there was also a strong inference under the earlier Acts that the mark ought to be either already in use or intended for use forthwith in an existing business in the specified goods. The principle, taken over from the common law, was thus that, since there could be no goodwill if the trade mark was not in use, there could consequently be no sustainable basis for an action for infringement unless the mark was in use. The 1905 Act's acceptance of a mark as valid for registration if it was 'proposed to be used' was a substantial and overt step away from the common law, and thereafter it was possible to bring a successful action for infringement of a registered mark that had never been used (though its existence could have been ascertained by the defendant by inspection of the Register), provided there was a *bona fide* intention to use the mark when registration was applied for. Trade marks not in use for a period of more than five years were liable, under another provision of the 1905 Act, to be removed from the Register on application by anyone 'aggrieved', whether or not the aggrieved person was a counter-claiming defendant in an infringement action. Nevertheless the 'proposed to be used' provision under the 1905 Act was more radical, and more

effective in creating a legal title and monopoly in new and unused marks by mere registration, than anything in the earlier Acts.

Word marks

From our digression to the 1905 extension of monopoly rights by registration (which were to be further extended in 1938, as we shall see) we must retrace our steps back to the 1883 Act. This Act repealed the 1875 Act, but was based on the same principles, though with elaborations and with one major development. The big change was the extension of registration rights to 'a fancy word or words not in common use', even if (in contrast to the requirements for registering word marks under the 1875 Act) not used before 1875. With hindsight one can see that this definition in the new Act was bound to give rise to difficulty of interpretation. The Registrar – or at any rate some of his Examiners – tended to interpret it as including ordinary words used only slightly fancifully in the context of the goods concerned, and in many cases to modern eyes and ears not fancifully at all. For example, COLOSSAL and SEBASTOPOL were accepted for the disinfectants and medicines classes, BRILLIANT was accepted for soap, starch and blue, NATIONAL for chemical substances, FAMOUS for common soap; and there were many other equally astonishing acceptances. The Courts, on the other hand, took a much more restrictive view, indeed leaning in the opposite direction. Such words as SANITAS for medicines, EMOLLIO for toilet cream, WASHERINE for soap and CARNIVAL for cigarettes were all held not to be 'fancy words'. It is possible that the extraordinary divergence between the Registrar (or his Examiners) and the Court as to the criteria for determining what constituted a 'fancy word' may have been one of the reasons, or indeed the main reason, for the otherwise unexplained removal from his post of the then Assistant Registrar soon after the Committee set up in 1887 to examine the working of the 1883 Act had reported. It may well have been felt that, although he personally had an excellent grasp of the principles and what ought to have been the practice of trade mark law, as is clear from the Minutes of his evidence before the Committee, his administrative control over the Registry's Examiners was inadequate. However that may be, it is no exaggeration to say that the 'fancy word' provision of the 1883 Act caused nothing but trouble, particularly as a result of the divergence of views and actions between the Registry staff and the Courts.

None too soon, a Committee was appointed by the Board of Trade in 1887, under the Chairmanship of Lord Herschell, to look into various matters of difficulty and complaint that had arisen under the 1883 Act. The Committee's final report was made in 1888, and its views and recommendations with respect to designs and trade marks were reflected in the new Patents, Designs and Trade Marks Act passed in the same year. Since most of the principles of the earlier Acts relating to trade marks were retained, it will be as well for present purposes to limit comment to what the Committee itself described in its report as 'the most difficult question which has arisen upon the enactment under consideration', namely that of 'fancy' words. In the upshot, and precisely following the Committee's views, the Act of 1888 abandoned that adjective and substituted 'an invented word or invented words', a definition

Examples of 'invented word' trade marks

BOVRIL	Beef extracts
ENKALON	Yarns and threads
FORMICA	Sheets of plastics
SANATOGEN	Medicated preparations
COPYDEX	Adhesives
KODAK	Cameras and other photo-graphic apparatus
HARELLA	Women's clothing
VYMURA	Wallpaper and wall hang-ings
FERODO	Brake linings
DULUX	Paints
BRITVIC	Non-alcoholic drinks
ERCOL	Furniture

which persists in identical terms to this day in the 1938 Act. Other words admissible for registration for the first time under the 1888 Act were 'a word or words having no reference to the character or quality of the goods, and not being a geographical name.' This definition also persists in principle in the 1938 Act, but in qualified and expanded form. In due course, after a number of decisions by the Courts, these new definitions of what word marks could be registered helped immensely to stabilise practice, both in the Registry and in the Courts themselves. Nevertheless, for some years the Courts were inclined to attribute to the new term 'invented word' the same meaning that they had attributed in their earlier decisions to the term 'fancy word'. Indeed it was held that the 'invented word' was by implication subject to the qualification imposed by the new Act on un-invented words: namely that it should have no reference to the character or quality of the goods concerned. As a result great ingenuity was exercised in ferreting out recondite or distantly allusive references to the character or quality of the goods in words which the ordinary, reasonably well-educated person would regard as having no practical meaning. For example, SATININE for starch was refused, as were, in both the High Court and the Court of Appeal, SOMATOSE for a meat extract and SOLIO for photographic paper. This inclination of the judges in the early years after the 1888 Act to interpret 'invented' by much the same criteria as had been used by the Courts in interpreting 'fancy' between 1883 and 1888 illustrates how slowly the climate of legal opinion, as well as of public opinion generally, adjusted to new ideas, even when faced with a new statute.

In 1898, however, the case for SOLIO was taken to the House of Lords, on appeal, where it became one of the first outstanding leading cases to set firm guidelines for trade mark registration practice. The Lords accepted the mark as 'invented', and their decision finally established that it was not essential that an invented word should have no reference to the character or quality of the goods, and that prior decisions on 'fancy words' were no guide in construing the substituted provisions on word marks in the 1888 Act. It had taken no less than ten years from the passing of that Act to reach these sensible conclusions. Lord Shand said in the SOLIO case that an invented word 'should be clearly and substantially different from any word in ordinary and common use. The employment of a word in such use, with a diminutive or short and meaningless syllable added to it, or a mere combination of two known words, would not be an invented word; and a word would not be "invented" which, with some trifling addition or very trifling variation, still leaves the word one which is well-known or in ordinary use, and which would be quite understood as intended to convey the meaning of such a word'. Lord Herschell in the same case, some ten years after chairing the Committee which had looked into the deficiencies of the 1883 Act, had this to say: 'I do not think that a foreign word is an invented word simply because it has not been current in our language. At the same time I am not prepared to go so far as to say that a combination of words from foreign languages so little known in this country that it would suggest no meaning, except to a few scholars, might not be regarded as an invented word'. The House of Lords do not appear to have been aware that the word 'solio' is a Spanish word meaning 'canopied throne'. It seems therefore that the word no more complied with what Lord Herschell intended in the first sentence of his test than does the well-known registered trade mark PERSIL ('parsley' in French) which is also accepted as an 'invented' word. Ignorance of the law may be no excuse, but ignorance of languages possibly sometimes is. In any case, both SOLIO and PERSIL make excellent trade marks, and if they had not been accepted as 'invented' they would doubtless have qualified for registration as words 'having no reference to the character or quality of the goods'.

Because of the SOLIO decision and others on similar lines, and the fact that the statutory definition, like much else in trade marks legislation, has remained consistent over the years (in fact the present wording is precisely the same as in 1888), the question whether a word qualifies as 'invented' has caused relatively little argument in the Registry or the Courts since the turn of the Century. Most of the arguments at the pre-registration stage, both in the Registry and in the Courts, have centred on deciding whether admittedly non-invented words, and in some cases devices (ie, marks which rely essentially on the visual impression they make), are sufficiently distinctive to be registrable; and whether marks, both invented words and others, are deceptive, either inherently (because of the ideas they convey or suggest) or by reason of likely confusion with other marks. There is an enormous number of reported cases under these three heads. The present book is written for the general reader, not budding trade marks professionals. Rather than discussing specific cases, therefore, we shall concentrate on the kinds of issue involved, naming a few actual trade marks by way of example.

Distinctiveness

Here we have two types of distinctiveness to consider: inherent, prima facie distinctiveness, and factual distinctiveness acquired by use of marks not initially distinctive. An important point about the second type is that some marks are not admissable for registration despite the fact that they have been proved beyond doubt to be factually distinctive in relation to particular goods, in that, by virtue of long and extensive use, they unquestionably indicate that the goods are those of a particular trader and of no-one else. The reason for refusal to register such marks – at least under the law as interpreted over the past twenty years or so (for in earlier days some marks were registered on the basis of acquired distinctiveness which today would be regarded as unregistrable) – is that it would be against the public interest to grant a statutory monopoly, as distinct from common law rights, in marks consisting of words (or the phonetically identical equivalent) which other traders ought to be free to use, not as trade marks, but purely descriptively. Examples of marks of this type which have been refused registration despite proved 100 per cent factual distinctiveness are YORKSHIRE, for copper tubing, and AUTOANALYZER, for automatic analysing apparatus. The concept is that marks which are established to be factually distinctive cannot be registered unless they have some degree, however small, of inherent distinctiveness on which to build. So, even highly descriptive marks may be registered provided there is sufficient evidence of factual distinctiveness acquired by long use in the market for the goods concerned, and provided always that they

Potato Crisps

Scotch whisky

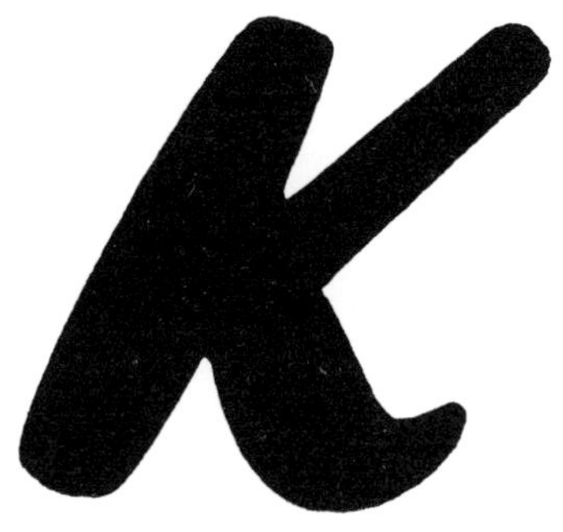

Radio, television and electrical apparatus

Boots and shoes

Motor cars

Paints

TYNE BRAND   Canned meat pies and puddings
TRAKGRIP   Tyres
MINI   Motor cars
STARTRITE   Boots and shoes
EZEGLIDE   Curtain rails
EVER READY   Batteries

possess an iota of inherent distinctiveness at the date of the application, which in such circumstances will of course always be some years after the mark was first used. Examples of highly descriptive marks which have met these criteria at the time they were applied for are HOVER-CRAFT (though this is no longer registered), for air-cushion borne vehicles, and UNDERSEAL, for preparations for inhibiting underbody corrosion on vehicles. There is undoubtedly a fine distinction between marks which are completely unregistrable and those which, although highly descriptive, nevertheless do qualify for registration on sufficient evidence of factual distinctiveness.

Consideration of the latter category involves taking into account all the circumstances surrounding the use of the mark in the particular field of trade concerned. More usually, marks registered on the basis of proved factual distinctiveness are not quite as descriptive, or prima facie non-distinctive, as the examples given, but are nevertheless insufficiently distinctive for registration as new and unused marks. Among the commoner types of this sort of mark are many surnames; marks consisting essentially of letters, frequently the initial letters of the applicant's name, such as M & B (May and Baker); and marks which, while descriptive, are not likely to be confused with an ordinary descriptive term.

Distinctiveness, as we have seen, is a prerequisite of registrability, and by far the greater number of marks registered are sufficiently distinctive prima facie to qualify under that head. Some are devices, which, unless they are representations of the goods concerned or are

not very far removed from mere descriptive
illustration, tend in the main to be inherently
distinctive. Some are 'invented words'; many
others are word marks which do not qualify as
'invented', but which are sufficiently distinctive
in themselves, either because of their unusual-
ness in relation to the goods concerned or because
such descriptiveness as they possess is allusive
rather than direct (for example, GUARDIAN
for locks, or SENTRY for burglar alarms); and
some are compound marks comprising both a
word or words and a device element, though
sometimes applicants are required to disclaim
any exclusive right to non-distinctive parts of
compound marks. To achieve distinctiveness
as such in devising a new trade mark is not
particularly difficult. Nor, in general, is it
particularly difficult to decide in the Registry
whether marks submitted for registration meet
the accepted tests of distinctiveness. This is not
to say, of course, that applicants and their agents
do not argue vigorously, and sometimes successfully, to persuade the Registrar that he is being
over-strict in applying these tests. Where the
applicant is unsuccessful and wishes to pursue
the matter, he has a right of appeal, either to
the Board of Trade or to the High Court.
Usually, however, if the Registrar maintains
his view that a new, unused mark is insufficiently
distinctive to qualify for registration, the mark
is amended to render it distinctive. Very often
only a slight amendment is needed, or sometimes the mark will become distinctive without
amendment if the specification of goods claimed
is limited, for some marks are distinctive in
relation to some goods but not in relation to
others.

**Examples of dictionary words having no
direct reference to the character or quality
of the goods and which are distinctive
trade marks**

SHIP	Matches
OLD HALL	Cutlery, forks and spoons
CARNATION	Condensed milk
LION	Eggs
HARP	Lager beer
GUMPTION	Cleaning preparations
BOOTS	Shaving instruments
JAGUAR	Motor cars
LUCKY STRIKE	Cigarettes
TUNES	Medicated confectionery
LOTUS	Boots and shoes
SURF	Bleaching and washing preparations

Deceptiveness

Distinctiveness is only the first hurdle. To be registrable, a mark must also be free from objection under both of the two aspects of deceptiveness: inherent, and that arising from confusability with other marks recorded on the Register. Here too the applicant can naturally dispute the validity of any objections raised by the Registrar when applications have been examined, and again there is both the right of appeal and the simpler alternative of meeting conditions the Registrar considers necessary to avoid the objections. Among the commoner conditions are limitation of the goods claimed so that the mark is no longer deceptive, or restriction of use of the mark to goods of a particular, specified geographical origin. Where the objection is on the ground of confusability with other marks, it is sometimes met by limiting the goods claimed so as to steer clear of the goods of the cited mark and also any similar goods; in other words, by creating a kind of no-man's land between the types of goods for which confusingly similar marks may be registered. Sometimes, where the likelihood of confusion appears not to be very strong, the objection is met by an undertaking by the applicant to give the owner of the cited mark notice of the new application when it is advertised, so that he can, if he wishes, formally oppose its registration. And, less frequently, where it appears that there is a fairly strong likelihood of confusion between the respective marks themselves, but (because of actual conditions in the trade, for example) confusion may not occur in practice, the objection is met if the owner of the cited mark supplies his written consent to the proposed registration. This last procedure cannot be used if the respective marks are identical; but identical marks can be

Examples of marks held to be confusingly similar for the same goods or description of goods

MOTRICINE	MOTORINE
petrol	lubricating oil
GALAXY	GLAXO
foodstuffs	milk food
ZYKOL	ZEE-KOL
disinfectants	medicines
EGALL	EGROL
dried eggs	egg powders
AMATA	AMAMI
toilet preparations	toilet preparations
ERECTIKO	ERECTOR
toys	constructional toys
KLEENOFF	KLEENUP
stove cleaners	stove cleaners
RYSTA	ARISTOC
stockings	stockings
ALKA-VESCENT	ALKA-SELTZER
tablets for making seltzer water	effervescent tablets for making seltzer water
MAGNETOPHON	MAGNETA
sound recording and reproducing apparatus	loudspeakers
VELVA-GLO	VEL GLO
paints	paints

registered for similar (though not identical) goods
if it can be proved that they have been in concurrent use for a sufficiently long period, even
in the same market. For this purpose it is assumed
that the cited registered trade mark has been
used, and, provided there has been no confusion
as a result of concurrent use, it is considered
permissible for the two marks to be on the Register side by side, even for similar (but not for
the same) goods.

Opposition

It is very difficult for some marks to surmount
all these hurdles and, as we have seen, impossible
for some others; but for the majority of marks
submitted for registration there are no difficulties, or only comparatively slight ones, barring
the way to acceptance by the Registrar. But
after acceptance there is the further hurdle of
possible opposition, provision for which has
existed since the first Act. All marks must be
advertised in the *Trade Marks Journal* before
they are registered, and, although only about
2 per cent of advertised marks are faced with
formal opposition, and far fewer still are defeated
in opposition proceedings, it is a gauntlet that all
must run. There is no statutory limit either to
the grounds on which an advertised application
may be opposed or on whom may oppose it;
but in practice oppositions are raised on the
ground that the mark fails to meet one or more
of the statutory requirements. Very many oppositions are based on the assertion that registration
of the mark concerned would be wrong because
use of the mark would lead people to believe that
the goods sold under it were the opponent's
goods and not the applicant's. The mark on
which an opponent relies for his case need not
be a registered one which he owns; quite a signi-

ficant number of oppositions are based on the
opponent's use of an allegedly similar but un-
registered mark. The opposition procedure provides a long stop for third parties to object to
the registration of marks, which, although considered acceptable by the Registrar after his
search for conflicting marks and examination,
are thought to be lacking in distinctiveness,
inherently deceptive or confusingly similar to
their own marks. The British system contrasts
with registration systems in some countries
abroad, where conflicting prior registrations
are not considered at all unless their owners
raise them in opposition proceedings.

Finally, if it survives the opposition stage (as
most do), the mark will be registered. Even then,
there are provisions, subject to certain safe-
guards, for a mark to be removed from the Register on application by a third party. However,
once their marks are on the Register most proprietors are safe from attack, provided they
continue to use them in what the Courts call
a 'normal and fair manner', and pay their renewal fees as required.

Distinctiveness and deceptiveness – how the one
can be achieved and the other avoided – and
the processes in general which a mark tendered
for registration undergoes have been discussed
here at some length partly to show the effect
of the law on individual applications to register
trade marks, and partly to illustrate that what
happens today is much the same as has happened
in the Registry and in the Courts for nearly 100
years. Certainly, discounting some aberrations
in the early years of registration, and the one
important development and four rather less
important ones referred to below, nothing very

much has changed, either in principle or to a large extent in detail, since the Act of 1905, or even for the most part since the Act of 1888. So as we enter the last quarter of the 20th Century civil trade mark law continues to reflect the attitude that the Government's function here is to hold the ring and see fair play between traders. The public is protected against misuse of trade marks by the successive Merchandise Marks Acts, and recently by the Trade Descriptions Acts, rather than by the Trade Marks Acts. Nevertheless, the public interest is served implicitly also by the Trade Marks Acts, for a mark which is inherently deceptive cannot obtain the advantages of the statutory monopoly which registration confers, nor can one which could be confused with other trade marks and so mislead the public who want the 'same again'. That trade mark law is concerned mainly with certain property rights of traders is further borne out by five developments in the law which have taken place since 1905. Only one of these is of major significance, but it has greatly increased the freedom of traders to deal in trade marks as items of property. One of the others makes it easier for traders to obtain the benefits of registration, and the remainder either enhance the rights of owners of registered trade marks or extend the range of statutory protection open to them.

Assignment of trade marks

The most important of these five developments originated in the 1938 Act, which for the first time gave statutory approval to the assignment of registered trade marks, whether or not in use in a business in the goods concerned, without the need also to assign the goodwill of that business. This considerable departure both from common law and from all earlier statute law was introduced on the recommendation of the Goschen Committee, a Departmental committee set up by the Board of Trade in 1933 to consider the law and practice relating to trade marks. The Committee took much evidence and deliberated with great care before making this recommendation. They concluded that, in the conditions of trade which had by that time developed, 'the goodwill' – in the words of a member of the Committee – 'rather attaches to the trade mark than the trade mark to the goodwill'. It was this proposition that was the essential justification for the change in the law in 1938, which of course enabled trade marks, once registered, to be traded in as independent pieces of property. The situation thus created would have been unthinkable fifty years earlier, but there is no evidence that it has worked to the detriment of the public interest; and it has certainly added to the value and attractiveness to traders of registering trade marks.

Registered users

Another change introduced by the 1938 Act provided for the registration of users of registered trade marks, so that persons or firms other than the registered proprietor could, in effect, be licensed to use a trade mark (though only under the proprietor's control of the quality of the goods concerned) without imperilling the rights of the owner of the mark. Before the Act these rights would have been at risk, since it could have been claimed by a third party that the mark, if used by persons other than the registered proprietor and with the proprietor's permission, no longer indicated a single trade source. The thinking behind the new provision was analogous to that underlying the introduction of assignments without goodwill, in that it was felt that no significant deception of the public was likely to occur, because, once a mark has acquired a good reputation, a proprietor appointing a registered user would have the same interest as an assignee in maintaining its reputation. Registration of users has proved valuable and has caused no practical difficulties.

Part B of the Register

The other three changes of any substance which have occurred since 1905 are relatively minor. In 1919 a short Act was passed whose principal feature was the division of the Register into two parts, Part A and Part B. Thereafter, marks which met the criteria of distinctiveness set out in the 1905 Act and were otherwise registrable were registered in Part A, while all others, apart from the most highly non-distinctive marks, could be registered in Part B, provided that they had already been used for not less than two years. The main object of the new Part B was to assist the export trade, since many British exporters were unable to obtain registration in foreign or Commonwealth countries without a prior registration, and many of their marks, although valuable commercially, did not meet the requirements of distinctiveness for registration under the 1905 Act. The innovation proved quite successful, and Part B was retained in the 1938 Act, but the Act replaced the registration requirement of two years' prior use by the simple requirement that for Part B registration a mark had to be 'capable of distinguishing'. Such a vague criterion naturally gave rise to difficulties of interpretation, reminiscent of the difficulties caused by the 'fancy word' criterion from 1883 to 1888. In course of time, however, and with assistance from guidelines in a number of reported cases, a reasonably consistent practice has developed, and relatively little difficulty is now found in deciding whether a mark qualifies as 'capable of distinguishing'. Since a Part B registration is easier to obtain than one in Part A, there is naturally a counterweight in the Act; Part B registrations never attain conclusive validity and can always (unlike Part A registrations after seven years) be attacked on the ground that they were not, on a proper interpretation, 'capable of distinguishing' at the time when they were officially accepted. Moreover – though this has not in practice proved much of an impediment to plaintiffs – a defendant in an infringement action brought on the basis of a Part B registration has the defence open to him that, despite his apparent infringement of the registration by reason of the use complained of, there is in fact, in all the circumstances, no likelihood of actual confusion between his mark and the plaintiff's. No such defence is open to a defendant in an action based on a Part A registration. Part B registrations have increased in recent years, and they now amount to between a quarter and a third of total registrations.

Defensive marks

There were two other new features of some interest in the 1938 Act. One extended infringement rights to cover the breach of a written contract between the registered proprietor and a buyer of his goods as to the manner or circumstances in which a mark is to be used. The other introduced what are called 'defensive' marks, which, provided they qualify as 'invented words', may be registered with rights identical to those of ordinary Part A registrations, but are not in fact used or proposed to be used in relation to the goods concerned. The idea behind this second innovation is that very well known marks, such

as TY.PHOO and OXO, should be protected
from attempts to exploit their goodwill by applying them to goods quite different from those
for which they are in fact used and well known.
Such protection is not available from normal
infringement rights, which are limited to goods
on which the owners of such marks in fact used
them and in respect of which they hold ordinary
registrations. Naturally, to obtain a defensive
registration it is necessary to provide very strong
and extensive evidence both of repute in the
mark concerned and of the confusion likely to
occur if the mark were used in relation to goods
well removed from those for which it is actually
used. Possibly for this reason there is only a
handful of defensive registrations, and very few
are applied for, perhaps two or three in a year.

Certification trade marks
Another category of mark which should be
mentioned is the 'certification trade mark'.
Registration of such marks was provided for by
the 1905 Act, when they were known as 'standardization marks'. Under the 1938 Act certification trade marks have to qualify under the general
statutory provisions for registrability (ie distinctiveness and non-deceptiveness), but their purpose is to certify that the goods to which they are
applied comply with certain characteristics,
whether of origin, material, mode of manufacture, quality or accuracy. The applicant for
a certification trade mark must not trade in the
goods of his claim and is required to show that
he has a viable scheme for licensing the use of
the mark to persons or firms who undertake to
manufacture and market goods which comply
with the characteristic which is certified. The
applicant has to establish – originally to the
satisfaction of the Board of Trade, and now to

that of the Office of Fair Trading – that he is
competent to run a certification trade mark
scheme, that the regulations governing the use
of the mark are satisfactory and that registration
of his mark will in all the circumstances be to
the public advantage. The 'kite' device mark of
the British Standards Institution, the 'skein'
device of the International Wool Secretariat
and the 'orb and cross' device of the Harris
Tweed Association are among the well-known
registered marks in this category.

Such, in broad terms, are the ways in which
trade mark law has developed over the last
hundred years. An enormous amount of detail
has had to be omitted, as well as a number of
substantive features of the law which are by no
means unimportant but which would have
distracted attention from the still more important
ones if they had been included. The object has
been to give some idea of the principles and
trends underlying the day-to-day operations of
trade mark law, and at the same time to show
that the essential requirements for registration –
that a mark shall be distinctive and not deceptive – have remained unchanged throughout. In
Chapter VII we take a look at what the future
may hold.

IV *History of the Trade Marks Registry*

If the reader had been walking up Chancery Lane towards Holborn before 10 am on 1 January 1876 he would have seen, through the archway of Quality Court, a small gathering of people waiting at the steps of No 4. The Trade Marks Registry was opening for business on the first day of the national service for the registration of trade marks established by the Trade Marks Act 1875. The service has operated without interruption ever since.

Although the pattern of streets and courts in the vicinity of Chancery Lane is much the same today as it was in 1876, many of the buildings have been rebuilt and have changed in character. The Patent Office, which had been established in 1852 to provide a single office for all the processes of patent registration, was situated with its main entrance at 25 Southampton Buildings, off Chancery Lane where the headquarters remain today. The south side of the office bordered Quality Court and it was here that the Registry opened its doors. Although there have been extensions to and rebuilding of the main Patent Office in subsequent years, and the territory occupied by the Registry has increased, it has always occupied rooms on the west side of the Patent Office building. Its present Public Enquiry Office and Search Room on the ground floor are located adjacent to Quality Court, where the Registry started. It must be one of the few Government departments to have remained as a complete unit on the same site for 100 years. In 1876, to the east of the Patent Office and on the south side of the garden court, were the Chambers of Staple Inn. Staple Inn was one of the Inns of Chancery whose influence as a training establishment for law students declined in the last century, and it eventually became a home for lawyers who had Chambers there. In 1884 the Society of Staple Inn sold the site, and the Chambers on the south side of the garden court were bought by H M Commissioner of Works for an extension to the Patent Office. Around the turn of the century the Office was rebuilt and extended with a frontage in the east on Furnival Street. The outward appearance of the Office, and indeed its internal geography, have changed little since the turn of the century, but the side bordering the Staple Inn garden was rebuilt with a temporary facade following the destruction wreaked in Staple Inn by a flying bomb in August 1944.

The 1875 Act provided for the establishment of the Registry not later than 1 January 1876. There is evidence that the authorities were hard-pressed to meet the deadline. The preparations for opening were rushed and little had happened before December. Mr H Reader Lack, who was brought in from the Board of Trade as the first Registrar of Trade Marks, with the duty of

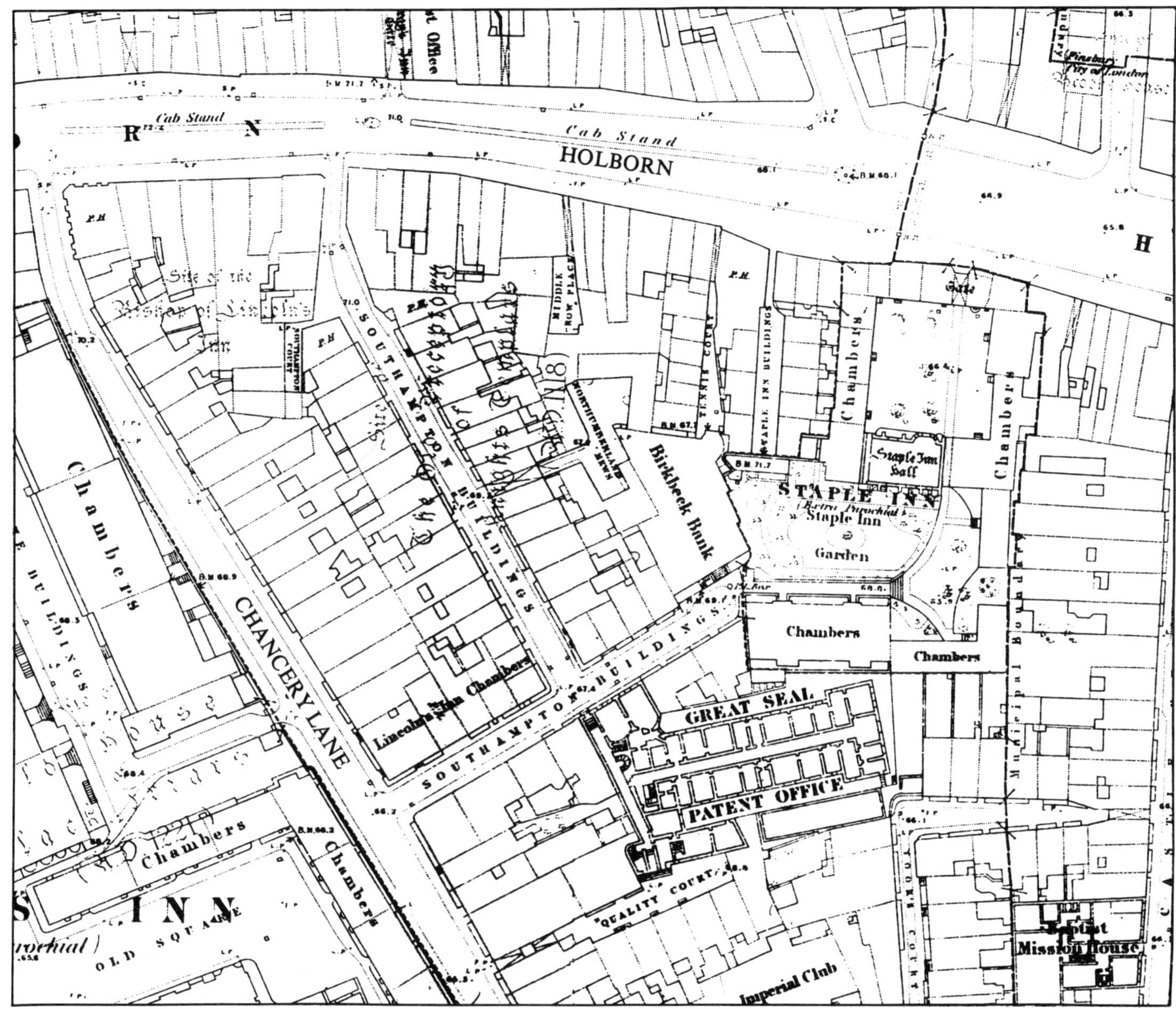

Map of the location of the Patent Office in Holborn in 1876

organising the operation of the Registry, confessed
to the Herschell Committee that he knew nothing
about the classification of goods on which the
trade marks registration system was to be based
until Christmas week. This classification was
founded on that used in the Great Exhibition of
1851, which was the nearest analogy that the
Treasury could find in starting the Registry.
Mr Reader Lack and his staff had little time to
consider it. It was drawn up after Christmas Eve,
was printed and circulated before the end of the
year and was on sale to the public with the Trade
Marks Rules by 1 January. The Registry's location was poorly publicised, and this brought a
letter of complaint to *The Times* of 25 December
1875:
'Having some important trade marks to register
for various clients we have made enquiries at the
Patent Office and at Stationers' Hall as to where
the new Office is situated but at both places there
is utter ignorance of the matter. Has it been
forgotten?'

It was not until 29 December 1875 that *The
Times* announced inconspicuously at the bottom
of a column:
'The Trade Mark Registry Office will be open
on 1st January next in Quality Court, 47 Chancery Lane. Mr H R Lack of the Board of Trade
is appointed Registrar...'

Despite the poor publicity, the word soon got
around and there was no lack of enthusiasm for
making applications for registration. Legend
has it that there was some jostling for the position
at the head of the queue on the opening day to
obtain the distinction of being the first applicant.
Trade mark No 1, went to Messrs Bass & Co for
their red triangle label for pale ale – a mark

Sir Reader Lack, First Registrar of Trade Marks 1875–1897

famous enough to appear among the bottles in Manet's painting of the Bar at the Folies Bergère. It has been periodically renewed by its owners over the last century, and is still registered.

On the first day, 79 applications were filed, and from then on applications flowed in steadily. By the end of January over 1650 had been lodged. Among the early applicants were J & J Colman, Charles and John Boosey, E Dent & Co, Callard & Bowser, the Procurator of the Monastery of La Grande Chartreuse, Thomas de la Rue & Co and Thomas Beecham. On 27 January *The Times* reported that the King of Saxony had forwarded applications to the Registry for registration of twelve marks used in the 'Royal manufactory of Meissen' for articles of porcelain and china, statuary porcelain, plaques, tiles and bisque china.

The Head of the Patent Office since 1864 had been Mr Bennett Woodcroft FRS. He retired early in 1876 and Mr Reader Lack succeeded him, combining the offices of Clerk to the Commissioners of Patents, Superintendent of the Patent Museum (later to be amalgamated with the Science and Art Department's collection to form the nucleus of the Science Museum, South Kensington), Registrar of Designs and Registrar of Trade Marks. He was a man not unmindful of his own worth. He accepted his appointment only on condition that his salary should be £1500 per annum, which at that time was, with very few exceptions, the highest remuneration in the public service. Somewhat reluctantly the Treasury agreed; but, by his labours and influence over the ensuing 20 years and more, he would appear to have more than earned his salary. His long tenure covered the formative years of the British trade mark registration system. He had to contend with many problems and difficulties in getting the provisions of the 1875 Act put into effect and developing the practices which the Registry was to follow in the examination and registration of trade marks.

The Act introduced novel concepts which had to be interpreted and worked out without the aid of legal precedents. It is not surprising therefore that in the early years there was considerable criticism from the users of the system as to the way in which the provisions of the Act and its subsequent amendments were being construed by the Registry. There were complaints about the criteria of distinctiveness which were applied in the official examination, and of the judgments exercised in comparing the similarity of trade marks. There were also complaints that the decisions of the Registry were inconsistent and arbitrary. Yet in many respects the Registry procedures introduced during Mr Lack's tenure were far-sighted and set the pattern for the way in which the work was to be conducted for 100 years. For example, the methods of indexing trade marks, whether words or devices, adopted for searching purposes have stood the test of time. Since its publication on 3 May 1876, the *Trade Marks Journal* has appeared in an unbroken sequence of numbered issues containing illustrations of all the trade marks (excluding certain marks for cotton goods) accepted for registration by the Registry, together with particulars of any subsequent actions affecting the marks and their entries on the Register. The system adopted enables anyone knowing the trade mark number and Journal number and page to turn up the illustration of any mark. Complete sets of the *Trade Marks Journal* are, of course, available in

I the Right Honble Hugh MacCalmont
Baron Cairns Lord High Chancellor of Great
Britain in pursuance of the Trade Marks
Registration Act 1875 Do hereby appoint
<u>Henry Reader Lack</u> Esquire of the Board
of Trade to be until further order
Registrar of Trade Marks for the purposes
of the said Act.

Cairns

The consent of the Treasury
is signified by

December 1875

Letter of appointment
of Henry Reader Lack
Esq as Registrar of
Trade Marks, signed by
Lord Cairns, the Lord
Chancellor

the Science Reference Library at the Patent Office in London, and can also be consulted in the reference libraries of the main industrial and trading centres elsewhere in the country.

Mr Reader Lack was aided from early in 1876 by Mr J Lowry Whittle, a barrister who was brought into the Office as Assistant Registrar of Trade Marks. His task was to assist in the interpretation of the new Act and in the operation of the trade mark system. This arrangement continued until 1880 when the Lord Chancellor, Lord Cairns, appointed him Master in Lunacy, whose officials, together with those of Bankruptcy, were at that time sharing Southampton Buildings with the Patent Office. A Captain Cairns (a nephew of the Lord Chancellor) was appointed to succeed Mr Lowry Whittle at the Registry, although there is no evidence that he possessed any qualifications whatever for the job. Towards the end of 1882 the duties of the Master in Lunacy were rearranged, and this coincided with Captain Cairns' resignation as Assistant Registrar because of ill health. History does not record that Captain Cairns was anything more than a sinecure holder, or indeed that he attended at the Office on any regular basis. On the proposal of Sir George Jessel, the Master of the Rolls, Mr Lowry Whittle then resumed his duties in the Registry and he remained in that post until 1888. Mr Reader Lack was knighted in 1891 and continued as Comptroller-General of Patents, Designs and Trade Marks (the title he had held since the operation of the 1883 Act) until his retirement in 1897. Thus from the time when the registration system was established there was a long period of continuity in the top posts. Mr Reader Lack and Mr Lowry Whittle worked together during the difficult formative years of the Registry and were concerned with two amendments to the 1875 Act: the Consolidating Act of 1883, and a further amending Act of 1888 resulting from the recommendations of the Departmental Committee of the Board of Trade presided over by Lord Herschell. Although the Registry was the subject of much criticism during this period, there can be little doubt that, if there had not been the continuity and experience provided by Reader Lack's and Lowry Whittle's tenures of office, the system would not have had such a sure foundation. After Sir Reader Lack's retirement, trade mark law continued to be unsatisfactory in a number of respects; but the changes which were needed were becoming identified and the general pattern of what was required was being worked out.

By the turn of the century most of the practices by which the Registry operates today had been developed. Indeed the procedures have changed so little that staff working today on files of marks registered long ago (which is often necessary in the case of marks which are still on the Register) have no particular difficulty in following the sequence of actions. Of course there have been refinements and improvements over the years in the way things are done, particularly to cut out the drudgery of the routine clerical work of indexing, form filling and the like, and to give greater efficiency in examination and other processes; but the Registry has resisted change for the sake of change and has introduced modifications to its system only when it has been thoroughly satisfied that they will have tangible benefits for the service offered or for the staff who operate the service. It is to the credit of the founding fathers of the Registry that they evolved a system which, in many respects, has stood the test of time and has been flexible enough for the Registry to provide a continuous service in the transition from the age of the oil lamp and horse-carriage to the jet age of today.

Officers of senior rank (now of Senior Executive Officer level and above) have, since the earliest days, been authorised to perform the functions of the Registrar under various provisions of the Act, including deciding whether or not marks should be accepted for registration. This is an important characteristic of the British system. Every applicant whose mark is objected to has a right to be heard, and most applicants who receive official objections to their marks take advantage of the ex parte hearing procedure to argue the case. Sometimes applicants appear in person but more usually they appoint professional agents, both to attend hearings and to handle applications generally on their behalf. The hearings before the authorised officers are informal in procedure and the majority of cases result in eventual acceptance of the application, usually subject to amendment, conditions or limitations. Only rarely does the hearing officer find that the objections are insurmountable and that the application must be refused. At these hearings the applicants or their agents have their cases decided directly by officers who are experienced in the art and who have the power to say yea or nay, and this system undoubtedly contributes to the rapid dispatch of cases. Applicants make very full use of the hearing procedure.

Right: Mr Edward Armitage, CB, the present Comptroller General and Registrar of Trade Marks, presenting the registration certificate of trade mark no 1,000,000 to Monsieur Doat, head of the legal department of the applicants, Pierre Fabre SA, a French pharmaceutical company registering the word 'Debrumyl'

In the Registry's first year, 1876, the number of trade mark applications filed at the London office was 10,384. After the initial flood the numbers declined in subsequent years; but between 1886 and the outbreak of the 1914-18 war they fluctuated between 8000 and 11,000 per annum. In the 1920s and early '30s – in the decade preceding the Report of the Goschen Committee which led to the current 1938 Act – applications averaged a little less than 12,000 annually, about two-thirds of the average in more recent years. Unlike patents' applications, whose growth reflects technological advance, trade-mark applications reflect the state of commerce and trade, and the rate remained remarkably steady until the mid-1960s. Since then the annual figures have risen, reaching a record level of 18,703 in 1972. The annual average of ex parte hearings in the Registry in the 1920s was nearly 4600. Today, although the possibility of registration in Part B without prior use has somewhat lowered the hurdle of distinctiveness, the greater number of registrations has increased the hazard of conflicting marks, and the proportion of hearings to applications is almost exactly what it was 50 years ago.

The staff available for manning the Registry when it first opened is another indication that the preparations were rushed. Apart from Mr Reader Lack and his secretary, the staff were all temporary, consisting of four Clerks on loan from the Patents Branch, one Clerk from the Office of the Committee of the Council on Education, five Civil Service Writers and two Messengers. (Mr Lowry Whittle did not join the Office until 18 April 1876.) However, steps were soon taken to put the Registry staff on a permanent basis, and, as the work developed,

more people were recruited, so that by 1892 the number had increased to 40. Today the staff of the London Registry totals some 180, which reflects the work involved, not only in dealing with the increase in applications, but also in maintaining the Register (which currently lists some 250,000 live registrations) and the search material which is derived from it.

One of the brightest stars to serve in the Registry was A E Housman. He was a Higher Division Clerk (at a salary, when he left, of £203 10s per annum) for ten years, from the time when he came down from Oxford in 1882 with a pass degree, to his appointment as Professor of Latin at University College, London. His well-known poem 'Bredon Hill' was probably written during his period in the Registry. Most of the staff had salaries well below his, for the most junior Second Division Clerk got no more than £70 per annum, and Boy Copyists – this was before the age of typewriters – considerably less.

Up to the first World War the Registry was a male preserve. By all accounts it was a monastic setting in which men worked for most of their careers without change of duty and with little chance of promotion, a situation which was to continue until well after the War was over. A retired member of the staff who remembers the first World War says that the Registry was staffed then by old men and boys, the old men being over military service age and the boys awaiting their call-ups. Some of the 'boys' never came back from the War: their names are inscribed on the illuminated memorial in the main entrance of the Patent Office. Most of those who did return spent the rest of their careers in the Registry or in other branches of the Patent Office.

A member of the Trade Marks Registry staff examining a trade mark application

Indeed it was characteristic of the Office until the second World War that staff served out their careers there. Between the wars there was little movement of staff between the Registry and other departments of the Board of Trade. The opportunities for promotion were few and far between; but most men were thankful to have a secure job in those days. Firm friendships lasting into retirement were struck between the 'boys' who returned after the first World War. A well known foursome were Messrs Whyman, Rouse, Handley and Cheesman, who spent most of their career together in the Registry. They all became Hearing Officers and all retired within three years of one another at the end of the 1950s. A large number of the staff were dispersed at the outbreak of war in 1939 to various expanding war-time departments. Charles Whyman went to the Board of Trade and distinguished himself in organising sea transport. As well as receiving a home award, he was decorated by the Dutch for services to allied shipping. After the war he returned to be the Executive Head of the Registry until his retirement in 1958.

Women did not serve in the Registry until the 1920s, when girl Writing Assistants were recruited. They were something of a novelty to the all-male complement, some of whom, it seems, were reluctant to have their cloistered life disturbed by female company. One of the earliest Writing Assistants to enter the Registry was Miss Joan Turner. She joined in December 1929, and was still serving in the Registry at the end of 1975. It is unlikely that her record of over 46 years' service (with a very short spell in the Patents Branch) will ever be surpassed.

Since the 1950s a considerable degree of continuity has been achieved amongst the more senior officers of the Registry. At the lower levels, however, there has been greater interchange of staff with other parts of the Department of Trade and its predecessors. This has had the effect of introducing fresh blood, and has given the staff a wider experience of administration work. Whenever possible, officers with trade-mark experience have been brought back for service in the Registry, very often on promotion. The overall effectiveness of the Registry has gained much from this policy, since it is linked with the continuity provided by the longer-serving members of the staff, which has seen the Registry through a great many vicissitudes. It has always been Registry policy to develop in the staff a sense of responsibility to its service to the public, and a willingness to provide as much assistance as is possible to applicants or their agents seeking to register trade marks. It is believed that all who have served in the Registry have been keenly conscious of this tradition.

Since the Registry opened, a large proportion of its business has been conducted with professional agents, who file trade mark applications, and deal with other registration procedures, on behalf of clients. The trade marks legislation provides for the recognition of duly authorised agents but does not specify who may act as an agent. Patent agents – members of the Chartered Institute of Patent Agents – have always undertaken trade mark work. In 1934, however, the Institute of Trade Mark Agents was founded by and for professional practitioners specialising as trade mark agents. The Institute has its own training schemes and examinations and lays down the observance of accepted rules of

conduct. Some solicitors also conduct trade mark
business, and members of the Patent Bar sometimes attend at hearings on behalf of applicants
ex parte, and, more generally, at hearings involving inter partes disputes. The Chartered
Institute of Patent Agents and the Institute of
Trade Mark Agents effectively and authori-
tatively voice the interests of trade mark applicants and registered proprietors on all matters
relating to trade mark law and practice. The
Registry places great value on the consultations
it has with representatives of the professional
bodies. With the spirit of co-operation which
exists, there are few if any problems which cannot be solved in a manner satisfactory to both
sides.

Nowadays an operator
records the particulars of
new trade marks
applications for a
computer data bank

V *The Manchester Branch and The Cutlers' Company*

The Manchester Branch

In view of the importance of the cotton trade in Lancashire the Rules to the Trade Marks Act 1875 made provision for the establishment of a branch of the Trade Marks Registry in Manchester to deal with applications for cotton textile marks. This Office was opened at 48 Royal Exchange on 24 October 1876. The Commissioners of Patents appointed Mr Joseph Fry to be the first keeper of the Manchester Branch, and he continued in this post until his retirement in 1901. The designation of the chief officer of the Manchester Branch as Keeper has persisted to this day.

At the time the Manchester Branch was set up a very large proportion of the cotton goods manufactured in Lancashire and in respect of which trade marks were used was exported. Many of these marks consisted of devices of animals, birds, reptiles, human figures, flowers, heraldic devices and so on which made an appeal to the eye, and were therefore easily recognised in foreign markets, such as Africa and Asia, where the buyers of cotton goods were mostly illiterate. The marks were used with small or negligible differences by many exporters because of their appeal to buyers overseas and the practice was tacitly accepted by the trade. Most of these marks had been used for a great many years and were well known as identifying either

different qualities of goods or goods sold in particular export markets, or even goods sold by different merchants in different export markets but produced by the same manufacturer in Lancashire. In the 1870s there were at least 60,000 such marks in existence, many very similar to or even identical with one another, and confusion was generally avoided by gentlemen's agreements between the British manufacturers and merchants themselves as to the particular areas where the marks were to be used.

The cotton trade was concerned about the implications if these common marks were monopolised by registration, for the Registrar's certificate would enable them also to be registered in the overseas markets to which the goods were exported. Therefore when registration of trade marks began in 1876, all users of the old cotton marks (ie those that were in use prior to 13 August 1875) were invited to send in representations of their marks for consideration by a Committee of Experts appointed by the Commissioners of Patents. The chairman of the Committee was Mr Edmund Ashworth, the President of the Manchester Chamber of Commerce. The 20 Committee members were all persons versed in the usages of the cotton trade. The Committee had the task of dividing the old cotton marks into two classes. The first class, or A list, consisted of marks thought sufficiently distinctive

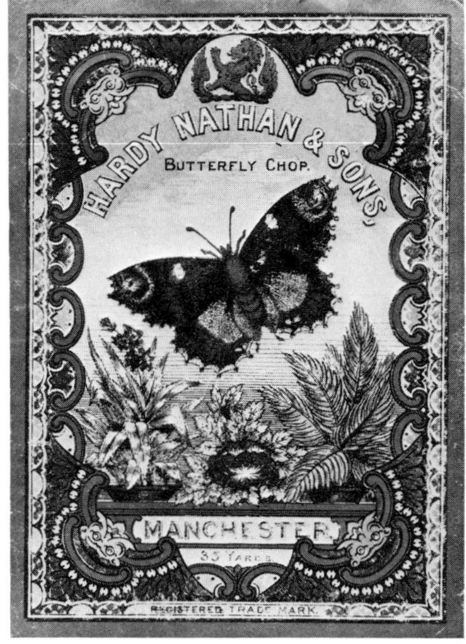

Representations of early trade marks for cotton piece goods

for registration. The second class, or B list, consisted of marks regarded for some reason as insufficiently distinctive, for example, because they were in common use, or little removed from marks in common use, or were not trade marks within the meaning of the Act. The Committee had a tremendous task in allotting marks to the two lists and its work was not completed until August 1879. It held 145 meetings in all, and sorted 44,218 applications, the great bulk for marks for cotton piece goods.

There would have been a greater number than this but for the fact that one of the largest firms, The United Bleachers Association, agreed to allow the whole of its 16,000 or so marks to be regarded as 'common' or 'open' marks. In addition to these, 37,614 marks were held to be in common use in the cotton trade and were allocated to List B. Only 3413 of the cotton piece goods marks considered were thought to be sufficiently distinctive for List A. In reporting to the Lord Chancellor on the termination of the labours of the Committee of Experts, Mr Reader Lack included the following acknowledgement: 'The Master of the Rolls desires me to say that his Lordship proposes that the thanks of the Commissioners of Patents be conveyed to the Committee, but it appears to his Lordship that when it is borne in mind that these gentlemen are engaged in very extensive businesses, that many of them have other public duties to perform and that they occupy too high a social position to be awarded any pecuniary recompense, the gratuitous sacrifice of time which they have made may perhaps be thought deserving of some expression of thanks from your Lordship on behalf of the Government.' This acknowledgement notwithstanding, it is clear from

contemporary evidence that there was a marked lack of enthusiasm in the Lancashire cotton trade as a whole for trade mark registration. Indeed most members of the trade were averse to it, on the grounds that the existing system of agreements within the trade worked perfectly satisfactorily, that the trade was largely an export trade in which statutory protection of marks at home would be of little relevance, and that there was a danger that registration could be used unfairly by some registrants to prevent the normal use of cotton marks by Lancashire traders in accordance with long-standing accepted custom. At least during the first decade or so of trade mark registration in this country there was a good deal of friction between members of the Lancashire cotton trade and the Trade Marks Registry, mainly because of alleged excessive lenience by the Registry in registering cotton marks thought by the trade to be too similar to marks of other owners. However, by the 1890s this friction had largely disappeared (probably less because of greater strictness by the Registry than because of the Lancashire trade's gradual acceptance of the fact of registration), but the number of applications for cotton marks became far fewer than in the early days.

Before the Act of 1905 the Manchester Branch had been authorised merely by the Rules. The new Act directly recognised the Branch and the Chief Officer was restyled 'The Keeper of Cotton Marks'. All trade mark applications in respect of cotton goods (yarns, threads, piece goods and certain made-up goods other than clothing) had to be made to Manchester, and the Keeper was required to make a report on his examination of them to the Registrar. Cotton marks

The staff of the Manchester Branch in 1901.
Mr Joseph Fry, the first Keeper, is at the centre of the
front row

which were registered were entered on a separate
Manchester Register, a duplicate of which was
kept at the Manchester Branch. The 1905
Act also gave statutory recognition to the Manchester Branch's practice of consulting the
Trade and Merchandise Marks Committee
of the Manchester Chamber of Commerce on
questions of difficulty arising from applications
to register cotton marks.

With the development of artificial textile fibres,
and of the practice of producing mixtures of
different textile fibres, there was pressure from
the trade organisations, at the time the Goschen
Committee was taking evidence, for the Manchester Branch to accept applications in respect
of all textile goods, including clothing. The
Committee, taking into account modern developments in the textile industry which had resulted
in artificial yarns, threads and piece goods being
no longer exclusively of Lancashire provenance,
recommended that applicants should have the
option of filing applications for trade marks in
respect of all textile goods and clothing either
at the Manchester Branch or at the London
Registry. This recommendation was embodied
in the 1938 Act. After the last war the substantial
development in production of man-made fibres,
with the consequent decline in the cotton industry, much reduced the importance of Manchester as a filing centre for trade-mark applications in the textile classes. The changing pattern
of the textile trade has led to nearly all applications for trade marks in the textile field being
currently filed at London. Only a trickle of
applications continues to be filed at Manchester,
though the duplicate Manchester Register is
still maintained there for public inspection. The
small number of applications received and the

cost of duplicating the records involved have
now made the Manchester Branch wholly
uneconomic, but closure of the Office is subject
to legislation.

The Cutlers' Company
The special position of the Cutlers' Company
(or, to give it its correct title, the Master, War-
den, Searchers, Assistants and Commonalty
of the Company of Cutlers in Hallamshire in the
County of York) as a registering authority for
trade marks for metal goods has been recognised
in all trade marks legislation since the first Act
of 1875. Long before the Cutlers' Company had
been incorporated by an Act of 1624, Hallamshire, which originally was an area corresponding
with the old Saxon manor of Hallam, of which
Sheffield was the centre, had been famous for
the manufacture of knives, blades, swords, scis-
sors, agricultural implements and cutlery wares.
The claim has even been made that the heads of
the arrows which won Crécy and Agincourt
were of Sheffield make. The duty of granting
marks in the Lord of the Manor's name was
carried out by juries of cutlers of the Manor
Court. The first known holder of a Sheffield
mark granted by this Court was William Elles,
who paid the Lord of the Manor a rent of one
penny a year for it. A document dated 2 October
1554 records that to the Court 'came one William
Elles and took of the Lord a private mark for
himself for marking iron knives, such a mark as
to have and to use by himself, and if any other
person should strike that mark and thereupon
be convicted by verdict, he shall lose to the Lord
twenty shillings and make amendment to the
injured party'. This early record incorporates
the rudiments of what were to become, over

Map of Hallamshire in
the County of York
*Reproduced by kind
permission of the Cutlers'
Company*

Extract of entries in the Register of pre-incorporation marks granted by the Cutlers' Jury in 1614

Reproduced by kind permission of the Cutlers' Company

three centuries later, the basic principles of
trade mark registration provided by statute –
an exclusive right of the proprietor to use a
distinctive (private) mark in respect of specified
goods with a remedy if the mark was infringed.
There was even it seems an annual renewal fee !
The Act of 1624 which incorporated the Cutlers'
Company stipulated that persons manufacturing
cutlery within Hallamshire or within 6 miles
thereof should mark their wares only with marks
assigned to them by the Company. It seems
certain that this early marking of cutlery wares
was not for the purpose of identification by
potential customers, but for the identification
of the maker by the Company, to ensure quality
and to hold the owner responsible for his work.
The duty of the Searchers of the Company was
to enter from time to time the premises of any
cutlers 'to search for deceptive wares and for
those that work, buy or sell contrary to the
statute'. The marking was for the good of the
trade. The concept of a mark as a valuable
property of the owner, and as an aid for selling
his wares and receiving repeat orders, was to
develop much later, when makers began to
appreciate that a mark represented a means of
identifying goods to potential customers and of
establishing a trading goodwill.

An Act of 1801 clearly recognised that corporate
marks for cutlery wares granted by the Company
were the property of the holder, and became
the property of his widow for life if he had not
transferred it by his own act through the medium
of the Company before his death. After the Act
of 1821 there was no restriction on the disposal
of a corporate mark by the grantee. In the first
national Trade Marks Act of 1875 the Cutlers'
Company retained its position as the registration
authority for cutlery marks applied for by persons
carrying on business within the Hallamshire
district. Subsequent legislation has, however,
taken away its status as an independent registering authority. The Act of 1883 provided for
the closure within five years of the Cutlers'
Company's Register of Corporate Trade Marks
and for the entry of these marks on a new Register called the Sheffield Register. This new Register in effect became a part of the London
Register and every application made to the
Cutlers' Company had to be notified to the
Registrar in London, to give him the opportunity of objecting to its acceptance. The Act
of 1888 applied all the statutory requirements
for registration of trade marks to marks registered
by the Cutlers' Company. On the recommendation of the Goschen Committee, the 1938 Act
gave persons carrying on business in the Hallamshire district the option of applying for registration of their trade marks for metal goods either
to the Cutlers' Company or to the London
Registry.

The name SHEFFIELD has long been synony-
mous with excellence when applied to cutlery,
steel and other metal wares. The Cutlers'
Company has been active in protecting the
reputation in this name against illegal use in
this country and abroad. In 1911 it set up a
Sheffield Defence Fund for the purpose of
protecting the goodwill in the city name, and
in 1924 obtained registration of SHEFFIELD
as a standardization trade mark (now a
certification trade mark) in respect of
all the metal goods for which the city was
famous as a manufacturing centre. The mark
has also been registered in a number of foreign
countries. The Company has played a long and

active part in the regulation and control of
trade marks used by persons in the Hallamshire
district and it still has an important function in
the industrial life of the city. Its role as a channel
for registering marks originating in the Hallamshire district has, however, declined since the
1938 Act. The numbers of applications filed
annually for the Sheffield Register can now be
counted in single figures. The bulk of the trade
mark work done by the Company now concerns
the renewal of marks on the Sheffield Register
and post-registration operations in respect of
such marks, for example assignments. In view
of the changing pattern of applications the
Mathys Committee, to which reference will be
made in Chapter VII, has recommended that
the provisions of the 1938 Act relating to the
Sheffield Register and to Sheffield marks should
be discontinued, though it also suggested that
the Cutlers' Company should continue to keep
for local reference, the relevant parts of the
Trade Marks Register.

VI   *Trade Marks as Footnotes to Social History*

All marks accepted by the Registry, except certain cotton marks, are illustrated in the weekly *Trade Marks Journal*, which has appeared regularly since 3 May 1876. A full set of the Journal's 100 volumes would now be extremely difficult to acquire. As well as being indispensable to practitioners, these 100 volumes, covering, as they do, one of the most significant periods in the country's history, are of great value to the social historian. Perusal of the million or so marks and specifications advertised in the Journal provides a unique insight into the changing patterns of trade and everyday life since Victorian times. It is not possible in the space available here to do justice to this rich store of source material for the social researcher: one cannot do more than dip into the treasure-house.

The Journal's first volume covers the year 1876. Looking through it one is struck most by the complete lack of sophistication in the marks of the day, with their frequent laudatory advertising content, occasional snob appeal, pride in the inventiveness of Victorian enterprise, simple draughtsmanship, and emphasis on the moral values of hard work, thrift and 'gentility'. Device marks were more common than word marks, reflecting a world-wide export trade, much of it to countries whose people read little and spoke English less. But, for the home market, applicants took full advantage of the definition of an unused mark in Section 10 of the 1875 Act which permitted the addition of 'any...words...' to the essential (distinctive) particulars. Typically Victorian in their flowery style, mass of information, engraved borders and decoration are those illustrated on the next page.

Royal patronage was claimed frequently and implied more often. There are dozens of representations of what is clearly the Imperial crown; a number incorporating the plume of feathers and motto of the Prince of Wales; and even some with the Royal Arms and motto, although the latter were not allowed on new marks. Labels would often lay claim to other distinguished patronage and recommendations, especially from medical men. Thus Dr Jongh's cod liver oil was 'approved of and recommended by the most distinguished scientific Chemists and prescribed by the most eminent Physicians and Surgeons (sic) in all parts of the world'.

Indeed, preoccupation with the state of one's health was very common and there were a very large number of applications for 'patent' medicines. According to one mark, the 'stomach is the seat of diseases'; a possible reference to gluttony being one of the seven deadly sins. Victorian references to parts of the body and their functions may have been bowdlerised or suppressed

OLD ENGLAND SAUCE.

Prepared according to the Recipe of the Original Inventor and Proprietor,

J. G. DEVEREUX

From the approbation this Sauce has received, the Proprietors are persuaded that it stands unrivalled for strength and fine flavour, and is peculiarly delicious with Fish, Game, Curries, Steaks, Cutlets, Omelets, Hashes, Hot and Cold Meat, Salad, Stewed Cheese, and all made dishes; also for enriching Gravies, Soups, &c.

Sold in Bottles at 1s. and 1s. 6d. each.

The recipe has been purchased by the present Proprietors from the original Inventor, and to prevent spurious imitation each bottle will bear a label, with the signature of the original Inventor and Proprietor, thus—

MANUFACTURED SOLELY BY THE PROPRIETOR AT HEREFORD.

in other fields but there seems to have been less reticence where trade marks were concerned. A mark for Holloway's ointment proclaimed that it cured ulcers and sore breasts. Others claimed even wider powers. CHLORODYNE was recommended on the label as a sedative for consumption and cancer and an antispasmodic for whooping cough and cramp, as an astringent for cholera and as a diaphoritic for colds. Such wide claims might not find acceptance under today's legislation. In the same vein (if you will pardon the pun) Dr White's composition essence was a 'valuable remedy for influenza, diarrhoea and cold feet'. No wonder the label stated it to be better than brandy! The curative powers of magnetism and electricity were widely believed in, not only for application to the body by apparatus but also by pills, one specification reading 'Electric life drops'. An application for the mark PARISS' PULMONIC CIGARETTES for 'patent medicines' shows that the association of smoking and health is older than one had imagined but not quite the relationship that today's Government health warnings convey. Sometimes these claims were not entirely free from ambiguity. What is one to make of Brand's essence of beef label which stated that 'in cases of urgent danger one teaspoonful may be administered as often as the patient can take it'? Signature marks were much in vogue. Their peculiar distinctiveness was much appreciated by traders anxious to avoid inferior products being passed off as their own, and many such labels contained the warning: 'Beware of imitations! Every bottle bears this signature, without which none is genuine'. Other measures to avoid imitations being substituted for the genuine article were sometimes indicated

in trade marks. One example on a mark for whisky was the injunction: 'Please to observe that the word KINAHAN is branded on the cork and that the seal and label correspond'.

Sometimes, but rarely, the advertising was more subtle. An example is a mark which consisted of a picture of a bear over the words IN MIND. In passing, it might be observed that a rebus makes a very good trade mark and it is perhaps surprising that more are not in use. A typical example of an outright message to patrons is Banks' trade mark, more than half of which is taken up with the announcement: 'F. BANKS takes this opportunity of informing those who sell or use his AWLS that they are manufactured of the finest quality of Steel, and hardened and tempered under his immediate superintendence and it is his determination that nothing shall be wanting to render them worthy of their continued patronage'.

One of the surprising things revealed by this first volume of the Journal is the number of applications for goods which are still with us today, often under the same label. Apart from the famous Bass label and others mentioned in chapter IV, there are: Ind Coope and Tennent for beer; Krug and Heidsieck for champagne; Martell's cognac; Rose's lime juice cordial; Glenlivet malt whisky; Stone's green ginger wine; Lea and Perrin's Worcestershire sauce (from the recipe of a gentleman in the County); Crosse and Blackwell's pickles; Colman's mustard; Keiller's Dundee marmalade; Huntley & Palmers and Peek Frean's for biscuits; Horniman's tea; Cadbury's cocoa; Nestle's milk food, et al. One could make a varied if somewhat unorthodox celebratory dinner from these

'centenary' products. The menu would of course be written with Stephens ink and the courses served on Minton china. Should any guest suffer from such an unbalanced repast he could seek relief from a box of Beecham's pills or Eno's fruit salt!

Apart from the almost complete extinction of domestic service, the lot of today's housewife is much easier than that of her Victorian counterpart. There is no longer any general need for such things as plate powder, polishing paste and blacking, for which there were many marks registered, one of them containing the eulogy: 'The servant's friend'. Somewhat surprisingly, though, she had 'soup squares' and, if she could afford it, a washing machine (sold under the mark THE HOME WASHER). In it she perhaps used the washing crystal advertised on page 139 of the Journal, stated to 'save soap and to be free from lime and other injurious ingredients'. Indeed, many marks were linked to products that were newly invented or improved designs of existing items. One such is illustrated on the left.

The smoker of the time usually made do with vesuvians, flamers and fusees, although safety matches were available, guaranteed to be without sulphur and phosphor, and which ignited 'only on the box'.

An interesting mark was that of the Post Office Tea Association (the origin of the widely held notion of the civil servant's favourite drink?) which had its initials in the four corners of a pseudo-postage stamp, after the fashion of the genuine ones then current. For those who suffered from tired feet, boots and shoes sold under

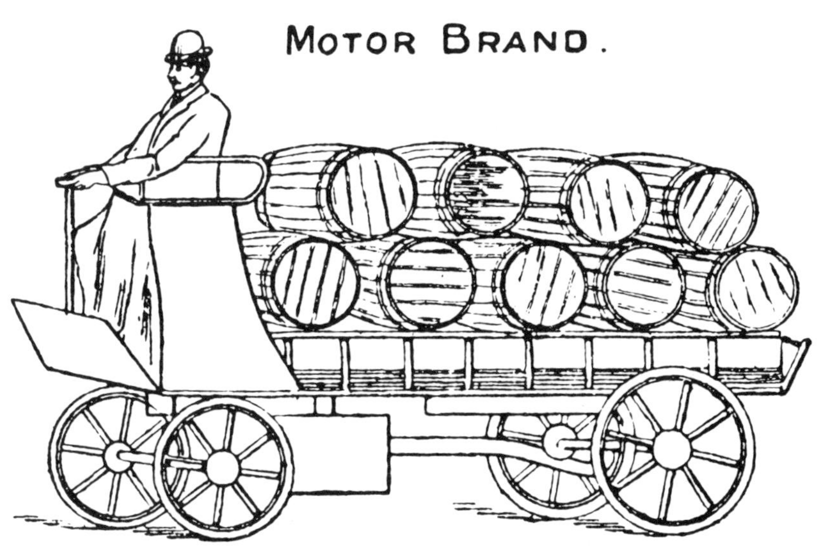

the mark WAUKENPHAST claimed to give 'Five miles an hour easy'. Members of today's Campaign for Real Ale may be surprised and even distressed to learn that a mark was registered for 'A substitute for hops'. While there were plenty of marks for drinks, there were remarkably few for foods, and what there were seem to have been mainly for goods sold wholesale. In those days most people bought their currants from wooden bins in the local grocer's, flour was weighed out from a sack, butter was cut from a slab and 'patted' into convenient shapes on the spot and milk was served by ladles direct from the churn. The days of pre-packed convenience foods were far off.

Symptomatic of the general belief in the essential unchangeable order of things are many marks which proclaimed their faith in the stability of the currency by registering the price of their products as part of their marks; one daren't do it today without a variation clause! One mark even contained a reference to a cash bonus of 3d placed in every sixth packet.

It is evident that the advantages of registration soon became widely appreciated, and by the turn of the Century the number of applications had reached 10,000 a year. Browsing through the Journal for 1900, it is apparent that the typically desirable mark was one that stressed the owner's up-to-the-minute style, preferably with an advertising 'plug'. The mark for cakes and biscuits (top left) of the New Century Cake Co must have presented itself to the public as a very modern combination. It is interesting to compare the vehicle with the one on the mark below left (for minerals), where the motor looks as if it was steam driven.

The mark for fly papers below looks very dated
today but advertises itself (twice) as 'up-to-date'.
The product sold under the mark on the right
evidently reduced the chimney-sweep's task to
a five-minute job for fourpence!

Some marks even included what is known as
'knocking copy'. One label for 'Virginian
Silver' stated it to be 'remarkable for its
absence of taste to the palate which charac-
terises German Silver'; but this did not prevent
its being advertised for a specification that
included both! One mark for a disinfectant for
'preventing the spread of contagious disease'
took the form of a graveyard headstone, but
whether this was a warning of the effects of
using it or of not using it is not known.

On the whole, marks were much less cluttered with non-trade mark matter by 1900, but extravagant claims were still made. A mark for a liniment specified it as 'a positive cure for wounds, haemorrhoids, bad legs and freckles'. There were many attempts at fancy (invented?) words, some of which might appear naive to the modern eye. Would LAFATEM for a toothache remedy find favour with a sales director today?

Among the more interesting goods, some of them fairly new to the market, mentioned in specifications of that year are: a lime cylinder for use with the magic lantern (the origin of 'limelight'); apparatus for taking and projecting animated pictures automatically; motor cars and motor cycles; pneumatic tyres; electric motors; electric storage batteries; typewriting machines and type ribbons; a talking machine; telegraphic instruments; electric clocks; electric lamps; fireproofing liquid; detergents; vacuum-packed tobacco; kid reviver (a leather polish and not a medicine for infants!). It is interesting to note a number of marks for 'macassar oil for the hair', a substance which had led long since to 'anti-macassars' being placed over the backs of chairs. A mark of interest to trade-mark practitioners that year was ORLWOOLA, advertised with a disclaimer to exclusive rights to 'All Wool'. (This mark was removed from the register by the Court of Appeal on the ground that it was not distinctive and was deceptive.) Products which have lasted though are: Angostura bitters; Schweppes mineral waters; Price's candles; Lambert & Butler's cigars and Brand's preserves (including game pies and boars' heads). Before leaving 1900 it is worth noting that some marks can be of interest to the architectural

historian, as can be seen from the one below (for cigarettes) which shows a contemporary view from Ludgate Circus towards St Pauls.

Each issue of the Journal begins with Official Notices. While these always relate directly to trade-mark matters they often throw an illuminating light on contemporary history. It is beyond the scope of a book such as this to show how the first World War affected the working of the Registry, but the following extract from a notice published in the Journal of 26 August 1914 shows that as far as possible an approach of 'business as usual' was adopted: 'As regards applications for . . . trade marks no distinction will in the first place be drawn between those made by such subjects (of any State at war with His Majesty) and those made by other persons. All proceedings thereunder will be carried on as usual down to the time of acceptance, but in the case of applications by such subjects formal acceptance will not be issued.'

The Trade Marks Act 1919 introduced the new Part B registration, for which applications were accepted from 1 April 1920. The first Part B application to be advertised proceeded to registration and is still in use. It is B402734, NUTTER, for 'fats used in cooking', and is owned by the original applicants, Mapleton's Nut Food Co Ltd of Liverpool, who have used it for nearly 70 years for a cooking fat derived from nuts and much in demand by vegetarians.

By 1925 there had been a tremendous advance in trade in consumer durables which was reflected in the products publicised at the Wembley Exhibitions of 1924 and 1925. Many of these new products are hidden in specifications covering the whole Class, but the following may be noted as indicating something of the wide range of new goods reaching the market 50 years ago: wireless telephonic apparatus; detector crystals for use in wireless telegraphy; electric condensers and transformers; radio receiving apparatus; cinematographic transparencies for exhibition; piece goods made from cellulose fibre; thermometers; capsules of gelatine for containing medicine; hypodermic injectors; headphones; pyrometers; canned meat and cereals for dogs; air turbines; thermionic valves; rheostats; electric welding plant; friction igniting devices for smoking pipes; windscreen cleaners; reservoir pens; iodised magnesia used in the preparation of salt for food (an early food additive?); dishwashing machines; bulb horns; stereoscopic pictures; time-controlled data indicators; safety razor blades; electric kettles; calculating machines. There were also some goods of longer standing, such as rubber teapot spouts; incandescent gas mantles; glass cleaning powder; acetylene gas motor lamps; bonnet brushes; hatpin stands; and button hooks.

Words were proving as popular as devices for trade marks for many goods, especially for pharmaceuticals, and much ingenuity was exercised in coining words that would be acceptable to the Registrar and still allude pretty clearly to a desirable characteristic of the goods. Two marks advertised in 1925 for 'medicines for human use' were BUKJUP and RE-NU-SU; no doubt both were tonics. A predecessor of WHISQUEUR was APRIQUEUR for an apricot liqueur, and ERLYBIRD has a certain felicity for a wormkiller. However, in contrast, SESAME does not seem to be particularly apt from a trading point of view for 'bolts, locks and fastening devices, all for use on doors and windows'. This was the age of the 'SUDSO' type of trade mark (still a favourite with authors). One notes the following in a single issue of the Journal: KLARKO; PUFFO; AVO; TIKLO; MARVO; SANJAMO; ALBACO; REMACO and FLOSSO.

However, devices still remained predominant in the textile classes because of the important export trade. Among simple line drawings of everyday objects used as marks on cotton piece goods were: a tin of sardines; a firegrate; paper on a spike; a bar of soap; a hot water bottle; a toothbrush; a biplane.

Two marks which seem to recall the atmosphere of the period are shown on the opposite page. The first is typical of the art nouveau style of trade advertisements of the twenties, and the other is a reminder of what washday Monday was like. An interesting light on the latter is thrown by the following directions on a mark for 'common soap': 'Cut up one Block to six gallons of cold water, adding a little Blue, then put the Dry Dirty Clothes in the copper and boil for half-an-hour, stirring occasionally. Do not overcrowd. Take out and rinse in two waters using Blue and you will find the linen clean & white. NB Should there be any scum use a little soda'. No doubt the clothes were then put through a mangle before being pegged out on the line to dry. Evidently this laborious process was the latest thing, for the mark also proclaimed 'NO RUBBING! NO SOAKING!! THE HELPING HAND – Its mission in life to help the housewife'. All in all, not a bad accomplishment for common soap.

Before leaving the Journal of 1925 it is interesting to note, in the issue of 29 April, the announcement of the publication of a Bill to establish protection for trade marks in the Irish Free State, as it was then known.

With the outbreak of war for the second time
in 25 years the same business-as-usual approach
was adopted as far as possible. In the Journals
for September 1939 notices were published
authorising the payment of fees on behalf of an
enemy in certain circumstances, as well as, in
approved cases, correspondence with an enemy,
via the Patent Office and an intermediary in a
neutral country. The war led to a number of
controls on trade, some of which were reflected
in trade marks. Many will recall the utility mark
CC41 used on clothing and furniture, but this
does not seem to have been registered as a
certification trade mark. One less well-known
which was, however, was WARNORM for
complete articles of clothing, registered by the
Wool Industries Research Association. A number of what might be called 'wartime' marks
advertised in 1941 provide vivid evidence of the
popularity with traders of marks which were
associated with anything topical. Among these
were: VICTORY handbags, PREFABCO
concrete buildings, HOME GUARD muslins
(for export), BLITZ sauce, BATTLE OF
BRITAIN jewellery, and the names of the fighter
planes which did so much to win that battle,
HURRICANE (for gloves) and, most popular
of all, SPITFIRE, for tobacco, overalls, cordage,
handbags, canned meat, fruit and vegetables,
cocktails and, perhaps most appropriately,
cooking fat.

The effects of the war were still being felt nearly
five years after its end and it was not until
6 January 1950, for example, that residents of
Japan could make applications for the registration of trade marks. But wartime scarcities were
diminishing, shops were becoming better stocked
and clothes rationing had been ended the previous year. The impetus given to research under
wartime conditions had led to many advances
in industry, and this is strikingly noticeable in
specifications, many of which referred to synthetic materials and plastics. These were much more
varied than the cellulose, viscose and rayon of
the 1920s and could be found in practically
every class of goods.

There were mouldable synthetic plastics for use
in manufactures, artificial fuels, artificial suede
leather, leathercloth of plastics, expanded
vermiculite, cellulose nitrate plastics, casein
plastics, acetole butrate plastics, artificial textile
threads derived from vinyl polymers, and among
the multifarious articles described simply as
'made of plastics' were flooring tiles, string,
luminous advertising signs, printers' blocks,
laminated sheets, bags, and articles of clothing.
Typical marks were coined to refer to these new
materials, eg NYLANA for a mixture of nylon
and wool, and PLASTICON for conveyor belts
made of plastics.

By this time too, marks for pharmaceutical
products, although as numerous as ever, consisted almost wholly of invented words with no
added matter. Instead of being 'cure-alls',
they were as often as not very specialised remed-
ies for specific complaints, eg: pharmaceutical
preparations for the 'treatment of amenorrhea',
or 'for use in connection with X-ray examination
and bronchography'. Sometimes they exactly
described their constituent drug, from which the
knowledgable might deduce their purpose, eg:
'pharmaceutical preparations containing beta-
halogenethylamine compounds for use in
chemotherapy'.

Trade marks were associated with inventiveness in other ways. An unusual specification from a Dutch applicant reads: 'apparatus for equalising potential differences on the earth's magnetic field for use in preventing injury to living organisms by earth rays'. The Registrar had no difficulty in allocating this to class 9 as scientific apparatus. This mark is no longer on the register and what sounds like a most useful piece of apparatus is probably no longer available. A sign of the times and a forerunner of the many food additives in use today was a mark for a specification reading: 'preparations of stearic acid and glycerine water white for use as ingredients in food as emulsifying agents'.

The propensity of traders to choose marks that could be associated with whatever was in the public eye was anticipated by an announcement in the Journal of 2 August 1950 that, 'in view of the forthcoming Festival of Britain and the exhibition of goods in connection therewith, applications for the registration of the word "Festival" as a trade mark will not be entertained'. This was so that no one trader could obtain a monopoly of a word that, at least for a time, would be needed by many. However, it did not prevent acceptances of marks associated with famous features of that exhibition, for example, SKYLON for stationery.

Browsing through the Journals, one often comes across marks that evoke a feeling of nostalgia, and 1950 is no exception. Visitors to the London Zoo that year would make sure that they did not miss the polar bear BRUMAS, and you may guess that this name proved popular as a trade mark. It was accepted for confectionery, toilet paper and fruit drinks among others. The comedian Tommy Handley died in 1949 but his fame lived on and ITMA was registered in 1950 for biscuits. ITMA incidentally comprises the initials of the Institute of Trade Marks Agents, to which reference was made in Chapter IV. The Institute claims no connection with Tommy Handley! An application for a mark for 'aluminium capsules for milk bottles' presaged the demise of the popular cardboard tops.

By 1975 marks were being advertised at the rate of 13,000 a year. One of the most striking features of typical marks compared with those of 100 years earlier, apart from the lettering and general 'style', is the essentially ephemeral nature of many modern marks. One wonders what proportion of them will still be in use 100 years hence. It seems that today's marketing manager looks on a trade mark as a direct aid to sales promotion rather than as a means of identifying the source of the goods. The latter function is increasingly performed by the 'house' mark and a practice is developing of using that in association with a more 'snappy' descriptive mark for each new product in the range as an integral part of the sales campaign. Most well established house marks consist of the firm's name that has acquired distinctiveness through long use and familiarity. Unless a firm already has such a mark it is necessary to choose one that can be registered without difficulty and the most popular choice is either a logo, the firm's initials in a cypher or monogram, or a fanciful letter device. In other words, today's house mark relies on design characteristics for its distinctiveness. The 'product' mark can then be fairly directly descriptive, although preferably still of a trade mark character,

and, if necessary, disclaimed. Typical of many
of today's marks are:
CADBURY'S <u>CARAMEL COMFORT</u>, non-
medicated confectionery containing caramel;
JOHNSON'S <u>WALL POWER</u>, cleaning and
polishing preparations for use on walls;
McVITIE'S <u>HOME BAKE</u>, flour confectionery, baked or prepared for baking.
Any right to the exclusive use of the words
underlined is disclaimed. This has led to a
proliferation of disclaimers on the register, a
development that is not wholly to be welcomed
since the public remains largely unaware of
them.

Another modern method of marketing is
for new products to be test-marketed before
being placed on general sale. Often competitors
are also in the field and it is essential to have a
mark that will be distinctive in its own right,
not only in case the product fails to appeal
(so that it has not become associated in the
public mind with the valuable house mark to
the detriment of the latter), but also in case it
succeeds, so that it can be marketed more
widely under the same mark on which much
time and money has already been spent.
Recent campaigns of this kind have taken
place with, for example, new smoking mixtures
based on cellulose as a substitute for tobacco,
and textured vegetable protein based on the
soya bean as a substitute for meat. It is not
without interest that products such as these
are frequently referred to only by initials
(NSM and TVP in the cases mentioned)
until they have established themselves;
further evidence of the wisdom of the Registry
practice of not regarding such letter
combinations as distinctive of any one trader.

Events such as the discovery and exploitation
of North Sea oil soon have an effect on trade
mark applications, and among those
advertised in 1975 were a number for special
'muds' or fluid additives used to lubricate the
drills.

There has been no room in this short survey
to make mention of marks for many other
discoveries and inventions of the past 100
years, nor to show how a study of the
advertisements can reveal much about changing
dress fashion, or indeed about many other
facets of everyday life. A fuller account must
be left to other authors and other occasions
but enough has been recounted, it is hoped,
to show that the *Trade Marks Journal* is not
as dry an official publication as it might
appear but is full of interest even to those not
concerned with the technicalities of trade
mark registration.

VII *The Future*

It will have been seen from previous chapters that there has been little change in the basic principles of trade mark law and practice over the past century, notably so since the major codifying Act of 1905. Recently, however, the registration system operating in the United Kingdom has come under scrutiny to see whether it meets the country's needs in present-day trading conditions, particularly in the light of international developments in the field of trade mark protection. Industry and the professional bodies have felt strongly that trade mark law and practice should be re-examined after the lapse of nearly 40 years since the Goschen Committee reported. In that time there has been a tremendous surge forward in industrial development. In view of the international nature of many trade marks there was too a desire that formality and registration requirements should be harmonised as far as possible. Indeed the need for the full examination and search carried out by the United Kingdom Registry was questioned when countries abroad appeared to be operating satisfactorily with something less than this rigorous procedure. In 1972 the Government therefore appointed a Departmental Committee which had the following terms of reference:

To examine the British trade mark law and practice and consider whether any changes are desirable in the light of present day trading conditions and international developments.

The Chairman of the Committee was Mr H R Mathys, now Sir Reginald Mathys, a Deputy Chairman of Courtaulds Limited. There were six members, representing legal, professional, industrial, commercial and consumer interests. The Committee received evidence from a great many organizations and individuals in the United Kingdom and abroad. Their Report was published in May 1974 (Cmnd 5601).

The Committee came to the conclusion that, whilst trading conditions had changed, the function of trade marks remained substantially unaltered as a means for enabling the customer to identify goods both for initial purchases and for repeat orders. They found that industry and trade regarded trade marks as being of prime importance in promoting home and international trade. They thought that the system of full examination of applications before registration in this country, leading to the registration of trade marks whose validity was unlikely to be challenged successfully, was desirable and should be continued. They recommended, however, that the distinction between Parts A and B of the Register should be abolished since the differences in the criteria

for registration were more subtle than logical.
They recommended that the criterion of
distinctiveness now required for Part B would
suffice for the new combined Register. The
only other major change recommended by the
Committee was that provision should be made
for the registration of marks for services
offered in the course of trade or business.
Trade mark legislation has applied hitherto
only to trade marks used in relation to goods.
The Committee considered that similar
provisions as to distinctiveness and search for
conflicting marks should be applied to
applications for marks used for services, for
example, repair services, banking, travel and
transport services. Other changes recommended
by the Committee were designed to simplify
procedures while retaining and strengthening
the existing benefits of registration.

As regards international aspects, the
Committee recommended that the United
Kingdom should continue to support
international treaties aimed at assisting the
flow of trade across frontiers by simplifying
and unifying procedures for the registration
and protection of trade marks. An important
development in this field was the signing of
the Trademark Registration Treaty (TRT as it
is commonly known) in Vienna in 1973. The
United Kingdom was one of the eight original
signatories, who included also the USA and
the Federal Republic of Germany. When TRT
is in operation (there has so far been an
insufficient number of ratifications or acces-
sions to bring it into force), it will provide for
the central filing in Geneva, by nationals and
residents of member States, of a single
application to secure registration effect for
their marks in any or all of the contracting
States which are designated, subject to the
requirements of the national laws governing
the registration of trade marks. International
marks for British registration received by this
route would be subject to the same detailed
examination and search procedures and the
same fees as British national applications
and may be objected to on the same grounds.
If there are no initial or third party objections,
however, or if they are overcome by the
applicants, the international marks would be
deemed to be registered under British trade
mark law. The advantage of the system is that
applicants wishing to register their mark in a
number of countries can initiate the proceedings by a single application with uniform
formalities and dates and the payment of the
requisite fees in a single currency. The system
would be likely to reduce the number of
direct national applications to the British
Trade Marks Registry by foreign applicants,
but at the same time to enlarge the British
Register at a greater rate than in the past.

Another possible development is the
establishment of a European trade mark
which would be effective, by a single
registration, throughout the countries of the
EEC, but nevertheless subject to the trade
mark laws of each member country separately
for the purpose of infringement actions.
Discussions are already taking place to work
out the principles on which a European trade
mark might be based. The Mathys Committee
stressed the desirability of incorporating an
examination and search system similar to that
operated in the United Kingdom in any
scheme for a European Trade Mark Register.

But the final pattern of the system which will emerge is by no means clear, since there are many difficulties in the way of evolving a European trade mark law which will meet the varying philosophies and requirements of member countries. The United Kingdom is keenly interested in the moves which are being made, and on 12 July 1973 it was announced in Parliament that the Government will offer to locate the proposed European Trade Marks Office in London.

It is evident from this brief summary of what is likely to be happening in the future in the trade mark field that after a century of established British tradition there will be new and more outward-looking developments in the future. Looking ahead, it seems clear that the Registry would be unlikely to be able to meet some possible future commitments with its present practices and procedures. The influx of more work resulting from the registration of service marks, for which there is likely to be a large pent-up demand when legislation is introduced; the possibility of more applications coming via the international TRT route; and the possibility of having to search the United Kingdom Register in respect of European trade mark applications: all these developments will require improved and quicker methods of record keeping and of searching for conflicting priorities. To this end a feasibility study has been carried out with a view to mechanising the Registry's operations. As a start the particulars of new applications are being recorded in a computer data bank. The next step will be to capture the particulars of marks already registered. This will be a long-term operation since the computer recording and updating of a quarter of a million marks and more will take some years to complete. The object is to evolve a reliable and accurate computer record-keeping system which will enable renewals, changes in the registration particulars, and many other administrative aspects of the Registry's work, to be dealt with quickly and accurately without the tedious and often time-consuming processes which are used today. Coinciding with the recording of the registration particulars in the computer data bank a study will be made of the ways in which the recorded data can be used in searching for conflicting marks as part of the process of examining new applications.

Changes in domestic legislation following the Mathys Committee Report, greater involvement in the international aspects resulting from ratification of TRT, a European trade mark system and the introduction of mechanization will all influence the Registry's work and involve the introduction of new techniques and procedures. It is clear that the start of the next hundred years will be a challenging time for the Registry; but there is among the staff enough knowledge, expertise and sense of commitment to the work for the future to be faced with confidence.

Registrars of Trade Marks

H Reader Lack Esq, 1875

Comptrollers-General of Patents, Designs and Trade Marks
Sir Reader Lack, 1884
Sir Cornelius Dalton, KCMG, CB, 1897
W Temple Franks Esq, CB, 1909
Sir William Jarratt, 1926
Sir Frank Lindley, 1932
Sir Harold Saunders, 1944
Sir John Blake, 1949
J L Girling Esq, 1954
Gordon Grant Esq, CB, 1958
Edward Armitage Esq, CB, 1969

Printed in England for Her Majesty's Stationery Office
by Burrup, Mathieson & Co., Ltd. S974050 BCS.

Dd 496561 K20 4/76